POSTCARDS

Little letters from life

DICK PAETZKE

Outskirts Press, Inc.
Denver, Colorado

The opinions expressed in this manuscript are solely the opinions of the author and do not represent the opinions or thoughts of the publisher. The author has represented and warranted full ownership and/or legal right to publish all the materials in this book.

Postcards. Little Letters From Life
All Rights Reserved.
Copyright © 2009 Dick Paetzke
V3.0

This book may not be reproduced, transmitted, or stored in whole or in part by any means, including graphic, electronic, or mechanical without the express written consent of the publisher except in the case of brief quotations embodied in critical articles and reviews.

http://www.outskirtspress.com

ISBN: 978-1-4327-2426-9

Outskirts Press and the "OP" logo are trademarks belonging to Outskirts Press, Inc.

PRINTED IN THE UNITED STATES OF AMERICA

For Adriana who has believed from the beginning and who will be my love and companion the rest of the way.

"Eyes are located so we can more clearly see things that are right under our noses."
                    —*Dick Paetzke*

Contents

Preface — 9
How these "postcards" came to be.

Caravaggio with ragù di salsiccia — 12
Italy. A tasty dish to set before a king.

Lux sit — 18
We are surprised by a bug on a mid-summer night.

La bella figura — 22
The fine art of not sticking out like a sore thumb.

Poppies — 27
A sad discovery and hopeful renewal.

Three cheers for the red, white and green — 31
Hurray for a childhood hero and juice on your face—and a controversial proposal.

Sempre dritto — 36
If you don't know where you are going, any road will get you there.

I hate airlines — 41
Every bit as comfortable as traveling by wagon train, although undeniably faster—usually.

"Lex" and other destinations — 46
Maybe why the lost city of Atlantis is still lost.

Today the cherries came in — 52
A traditional arrival, and visitors, welcome and un.

La botola   58
Life is not a cabaret, old chum, it is a trapdoor in an Italian game show.

The moon is full   63
If you think that's an ordinary event, you don't understand the gravity of the situation.

Men are Vespas, women are Valentines   69
World peace as close as your kitchen cupboard.

Dutch   75
Words are not enough.

It's a dog's life   78
A story with a varied cast of characters and many legs.

The intern   84
I almost make a mistake. A tale of friendship, love, and a blind man.

Pancake makeup   87
How to make a lot of dough in interior decorating.

The advent   91
A Scrooge-less tale of a different time.

Love, Joey   97
A little kid pulls me out of a deep hole.

Read any good books lately?   101
An obsession confession.

Wing tips   107
How a duck gave aeronautical engineers the bird.

Whatever happened to holidays? 110
Have we watered down their punch?

Cogito ergo zoom 116
Living life on two wheels.

Open season 121
What's your sign? Orvis or Cabela's?

The tenants 128
We adopt a flighty family.

Grandpas "R" us 134
I lose my mind and my carefully protected identity.

Life without eyebrows 141
A revealing exploration through the looking glass.

You are where you eat 146
Excuse me fly, there's a waiter in my soup.

The Trojan horse 153
Unwitting inhabitants conquered by a superior force.

"...those things which make us human are, curiously enough, always close at hand. "
—Walt Kelly

Preface

"Hello big boy
how are you
be a good Boy till
daddy gets back
daddy"

The writing in pencil was loopy and not punctuated, betraying the fact that my father had only an elementary school education in Germany. Even that was interrupted at age 12 when he was sent alone to the United States to live with an uncle and then make his own way in life.

Making his way was still what he was doing when the mailman delivered his postcard to me. It was written during the heart of America's Great Depression in a cheap hotel room in the tiny town of Everson, Washington, many miles away from where we lived in Seattle. A boilermaker with powerful muscles and work hardened hands, my father often traveled far to bring home meager earnings to help stretch the food he and my mother grew in our garden. At age four, I didn't know that we were poor. But I did know that my father loved me. The postcard that my mother read to me told me so.

Others followed. Many were no more verbose than those 15 words and a picture I have saved forever. They started coming for my first birthday, some from relatives in Germany that I would not meet for decades. An aunt sent me a dramatic postcard of a pre-war Zeppelin she had traveled on, now a forgotten cruise ship of the sky, almost as mythical as a unicorn.

My brother, in the Army at the end of the Second World War, flooded the mail with almost daily postcards connecting all of us at home with his life and reassuring us that he was safe and well.

Over the years, postcards flew among us with friends and relatives and people important to us. Scenes of Mt. Rainier, the Empire State building, oil rigs on California's Sunset Hill, monuments in Europe, beaches in Hawaii, campgrounds in forests, fields of wheat, sunflowers and corn. All bore messages that said, "Here is part of my life, I'd like to share it with you because your life and mine are woven together in a way that feels good."

I even still have a postcard of the Hotel Governor Clinton opposite Pennsylvania station in New York. *(All Outside with Private Bath, Radio, Television, Servidor and Circulating Ice Water.)* It is otherwise blank and unmailed. I may have even intended to send it to someone, but what 23-year-old soldier on his one-night honeymoon at the end of a ten-day leave sends anybody a postcard? And can anyone tell me what a Servidor is?

If postcards have a shortcoming however, it is lack of space. There's usually barely room for "having a wonderful time..." When my wife, Adriana, and I started traveling almost annually to a family home in southern Italy, my life was suddenly full of new images and new experiences. Too much for a souvenir store postcard, so I created one or two of my own. The Internet became my mailman. And my postcards became more than greetings.

I sincerely hope you like what you see here. You will find more here than just travel observations and much of it has nothing to do with that subject at all. They are all simply little letters from life. And that happens wherever you are.

I am betting that my life is not all that different from yours. I hope my "postcards" will entertain you, connect with your heart, and perhaps mirror the kinds of moments that have touched and changed you too.

Caravaggio with ragù di salsiccia. Delicious!

What a country this is! Some weeks back, we spent a couple of days in Rome with our friend, Ricardo de Mambro Santos. A Brazilian who came to study at the University of Rome at 17, he stayed on to become a distinguished teacher of art history at this ancient institution.

He'd already called our hotel before we arrived and after we'd checked in met us in the lobby. "Adriana! Dick! I am so happy to see you," he cried as he threw his arms around my bride. He has been writing her e-mails filled with passionate sounding endearments that only a Latin would write to a married woman, without fear of being shot. I could only smile with pleasure at seeing him, because that's Ricardo and we both love him.

He'd promised to show us things in Rome that we'd never seen. "Everywhere you look in Rome, every corner, every building, every nook and cranny, there is art and history," he declared. "There's so much that we'll just focus on things we can walk to right around your hotel."

"Hmm. Quick tour," I thought. Was I ever wrong. I already knew that the most obvious thing in the neighborhood was the Pantheon a block and a half away. But we immediately charged off to Santa Maria sopra Minerva, a beautiful church built long ago on top of the remains of a pagan Roman temple. We'd already been there a dozen times before and both loved Michelangelo's statue of Christ bearing his cross.

"Been there, done that," I muttered. But Ricardo stopped at the doorway and pointed up at an old inscription with a line under it high up high on the wall. There were similar ones a foot or two lower. "High water marks," he explained. "The Tiber River used to flood. Imagine how much art was lost in those floods." The marks were at least six feet above our heads and maybe 16 to 18 feet above the street surface!

Plunging into the church, we got an art history lesson at every painting, pillar and icon—and they were countless. At last we came to Michelangelo's Christ, which of course I already knew all about. Ha. Ha.

"Of course, this is likely not really the work of

Michelangelo," Ricardo related. "He started on it and discovered the block of marble he was working on had a disfiguring black vein running through it. He apparently abandoned the work." What we were looking at was apparently a second work done by somebody else and exhibits sculptural characteristics that weren't typical of the master. I knew that of course, just as you did.

I made some inappropriate remark about the Lord's fig leaf. "The conventional wisdom," Ricardo said, "was that it was added during the Reformation. It's not true." He told us it was added in the 1930s by Mussolini's government that lopped off the divine appendage to protect public morality.

"What did they do with it?" I said, sensing the immense value of such a sensational find sometime in the future. "That's one of art's enduring mysteries," Ricardo noted as we talked about working together on a novel that would put the DaVinci code to shame.

Our tour, which took us the better part of two days and ran my legs off, took us to the gorgeous Galleria Doria Pamphilij with its own version of Versailles' Hall of Mirrors and hundreds upon hundreds of masterworks and then on to the Oratorio di Santa Croce where Ricardo showed us huge paintings by Caravaggio, who revolutionized art techniques with his stunning use of light, shadow, color and dramatic action. Pre-Ricardo it would have been a 15-minute walk-through. This time it was human history come to life and I have no idea how long we were there. That was all in a few square blocks.

If the richness that is art in Italy is such an immense and unbelievably deep expression of a country's soul and perhaps that of mankind, the only thing that comes close isn't in a church or a gallery. It's in a ristorante, trattoria, osteria, or in an Italian home, where people are sitting down to eat.

Recipes are not in magazines or cookbooks, they are first in people's hearts and their genes. Tomorrow Adriana has been invited to a lady's home, a friend of a friend, to learn how to hand make *orrecchiette*, delicate "little ears" of pasta, the size of coins. The secret, never truly fathomed by Barilla or Chef Boyardee, is passed along by men and women who learned from parents and grandparents. Handmade orrecchiette and a fine sauce are a tender delight without equal.

In the nearby Osteria degli Spiriti I was served *ceceri con tria*, a puree of ceci beans—long, green vegetable-based strips of pasta the width of a man's belt. I had to let mine out a notch, and if you had offered me chateaubriand, I would have turned you down cold.

Over on the other side of this peninsula, which is the "heel" of the Italian boot, a restaurant in Gallipoli, La Puritate, features seafood, most of which is fetched out of the sea about 50 yards away. I don't like everything that falls under the umbrella of seafood and here that includes a lot of creatures, from sea urchins to swordfish. I have a personal rule for example never to put anything in my mouth that has, or once had, suction cups on it. Adriana had a seafood salad glistening with beautiful white rings of calamari and loaded with mussels dripping golden oil and I had to confess it looked pretty tempting. I settled for risotto con gamberi, tender prawns that someone had mercifully peeled, which isn't always the case here. Sensational. Plus, I sneaked some deep-fried *alici* off her plate, little inch and a half long sardines, crisp and scrumptious. I even looked them in the eye and apologized as I popped them into my mouth.

Last week we looked for a new restaurant that we had discovered two years ago in Ostuni, about an hour from here in Lecce. We had almost given up on finding it again, when we realized that not only the name of the street had disappeared but the restaurant already had a new name and new owners. "Oh, what the heck," we thought. "We've come this far."

Write down the name, Le Mura, if you ever plan to visit Ostuni. It's a family place, a mother and two sons. One son, young Arcangelo Gioia is the chef. A rough translation of his name would be "archangel of joy." That will give you an idea about the menu brought to us by his younger brother, Gianluca. We ordered their fixed price "traditional Apulian dishes."

Our ecstasy began with an incredibly delicate warm puree of fave beans with a hot flan of vegetables in season. It was followed by orrecchiette made by hand and a sauce with farm style "firm" ricotta. On the heels of that a mixed meat ragù with tiny "meatballs" of lightly deep fried potato. In and around that we were brought wine, appetizers, tiny chocolates, pastries, limoncello and coffee. After dinner we rushed to the kitchen to meet mamma, a tiny, young, and pretty woman who didn't look at all like what I had expected. The *Joy* family. Artists.

I could go on about the people we meet who know more about cooking than anybody I know. Some are professionals and in the business of preparing savory food, but many others are just men and women like you and we are. I'd just make you hungry.

Italy is about art in forms that dazzle the senses. It is not like Hawaii or Mexico or Thailand or France or other places you may wander. Neither is it perfect or a paradise. But what is here is mighty tasty.

Gorge yourself.

Dick

Lecce, Italy

Lux sit

And God said, "Let there be light" and there was light. He must have thought it was such a good idea that He didn't have to explain how He did it. Nevertheless, it kept us from trying to read in the dark.

Striving mightily to keep struggling University of Washington students from being in the dark, an early president of that institution adopted the Almighty's directive and plastered it in Latin on the school's seal, even though Latin came along quite a lot later than God's effort did.

One of the students who got illuminated was my wife Adriana, who found herself in an Italian class taught by Erminia Ardissino, a *professoressa* imported from la bella Italia. Adriana thrived under her teaching, grew in her skills and built a warm and caring relationship with her fine teacher. Which was why we found ourselves some time later trying to find the country home in Cigliano some kilometers from Turin where Erminia lived with her painter husband. We'd been invited for the day and had scrupulously followed her directions on how to get there from our hotel in Milan. After a pleasant lunch Erminia took us touring in Turin where some kind of festival event happened to be going on involving the famous "Shroud of Turin," believed by many to be the actual burial cloth of Christ, and bearing what looks to be an imprint of a crucified man. While we didn't see the Shroud, we saw plenty of Shroud T-shirts, which somehow fell short of being soul-stirring.

Though we got back to Cigliano late and knew we'd be getting home even later, Erminia insisted on preparing a wonderful dinner. We were stuffed with fine food and wine and it was gathering dark when we walked around the corner of the house on our way to our car parked in front. Suddenly I stopped short at the yard gate, stunned.

The gate was ablaze with brilliant white Christmas lights. I stepped back, this was summer, how could this be? But the lights were suddenly all over, intense blue white—*and they were moving!* They were hovering over our car and filled the field across the street, and clinging to the blades of grass and stalks of weeds. *Fireflies.*

If you come from someplace where there are

fireflies, you have to forgive my amazement. They don't exist where we live in the Pacific Northwest and neither of us had ever seen one. And here there were thousands. "They are *luciole*," Erminia explained in response to my, "Uh, uh, wha...??" (A poised and articulate query, if I ever heard one.)

I held my breath and even today my heart starts beating faster when I recall that sight, to me a miracle and one of the most beautiful things I have ever seen.

It made me seriously re-think my relationship with bugs, though most still haven't moved up much in my esteem, especially flies and mosquitoes. (Italians call mosquitoes *zanzare*, which sounds exactly like the "ready or not, here I come" buzz they make before they attack you in bed.)

I know the ecologists and theologians, too, tell us that all things on this earth are there for a purpose. I don't think that *luciole* have been put here to read by. They are too much like some other things I have seen and heard in Italy attached to names such as Michelangelo, Bernini, Puccini and that honorary Italian, Wolfgang Amadeus whatshisname. Things that give you goose bumps. If you throw in *orata* baked in a thick crust of salt, Negroamaro wine from Puglia, and fresh figs for breakfast, it is hard to find that much astonishment in one place.

We got lost on our way back to Milan. It took us an hour to get there and almost two hours to find our hotel. We passed the same dark corner in Milan and the same bright covey of skimpily dressed prostitutes three times before we decided we now knew them well enough to make friends and ask for directions. As is usual in Italy, they told us, "*Sempre dritto,*" straight ahead. We got there anyway, marveling at our whole adventure, maybe not as big as landing on the moon, but certainly illuminating.

Fireflies go by a variety of names, including "lightning bugs," and "glowworms." A long time ago I was fortunate enough to be able to interview the legendary Mills Brothers who sang their hit "The Glow-worm:"

> *Shine little glow-worm, glimmer, glimmer.*
> *Shine little glow-worm, glimmer, glimmer.*
> *Lead us lest too far we wander.*
> *Love's sweet voice is calling yonder.*
> *Shine little glow-worm, glimmer, glimmer.*
> *Hey, there don't get dimmer, dimmer.*
> *Light the path below, above.*
> *And lead us on to love!*

Lux sit. Let there be light and may it shine on you and those you love, filling you with amazement at this world we live in.

Dick

Lecce, Italy

While this is a bella figura it is not La Bella Figura

La bella figura
Don't leave home without it

The sole purpose of this postcard is to save you from yourself should you ever travel to Italy. It was inspired by a trip to the beach yesterday and the non-inspiring sight of three overly large German lady tourists who talked loudly and incessantly for the entire four hours we were there.

If there is one thing Italians prize above all else it is the art of fitting in, being graceful, well-turned out, highly regarded by others and always thought of as doing the right thing, looking the right way, and behaving in a way that is "approved" by everybody.

The Italians call that state of personal being *la bella figura*, loosely "the beautiful figure." It is why most Italians dress to the nines, don't wear fanny packs, and only recently started wearing shorts in the city. A couple of years ago they were considered something one wore only at the beach.

Many *americani* couldn't care less, which is why in Italy we often stick out like proverbial sore thumbs, bumpkins, bozos, dorks or idiot children. Or in extreme cases, Ugly Americans who just climbed out of the RV.

The rules of *la bella figura* are simple, but countless beyond number. Here are some:

It is always better to dress like you work in Manhattan, than like you play in a garage band in Seattle.

Don't order "dipping oil" for your bread. And also forget the "fettucini Alfredo." If you find the former in Italy, it's only because so many bozos have asked for it in tourist restaurants. The latter is a New York invention and not Italian.

Don't ask for parmesan cheese for your penne with scampi. Italians never eat cheese with seafood, even if it's tiny shrimp tucked in your risotto.

Don't order pizza in a restaurant before evening meal time. In most non-tourist places they don't make it during the day.

Don't drive in the passing lane. Honk or blink your lights, pass and then get the hell out of the way. There are no other rules regarding driving in Italy except getting the hell out of the way. This is also a basic rule if you are a pedestrian and may be a key to survival.

Keep your voice down. If you are a teenager, consider traveling to a different country or staying at home.

Don't drink like Dean Martin. *La bella figura* is one reason most Italians are moderate about both eating and drinking. The worst thing that could happen is that someone thought you were out of control. It is okay to be out of control only if it involves soccer.

Forget your Iced Quad Venti Sugar-Free Vanilla Nonfat with Whip Caramel Macchiato. I have heard there is now a Starbucks in Milan, but, if so, it is a lonely outpost. The Italians love their own coffee and it's laden with tradition, not bizarre choices. Cappuccino is drunk only at breakfast. Ask for it in the afternoon at your own risk.

Run if you must, but do it before everybody else is up. Most Italians wouldn't be caught dead jogging or running in what looks like their underwear. I have never seen a gym in Italy, though I understand there are some. Only a rare Italian woman would ever let anyone see her sweating on a Stairmaster in the front window of a health club. Ewww!

Titles are important. Not "Your Majesty" or "Contessa," but the ones that go with common courtesy—*signore, signora, signorina*. Pretend you went to a southern military school and call your father "sir" and say "yes, ma'am" to your mother. Don't call people by their first names unless you've been invited to do so.

Don't "ciao" people you don't know. It's a greeting used among friends. It's not like being in a restaurant here, where "Hi-I'm-Bob-Your-Server" immediately becomes your close friend. Italians are much more private. That does not mean however, that they are not extremely nosy and judgmental about what they regard as bozo-ism in others.

Stuffy, you say? Maybe you're right. But it's mostly a matter of being more cognizant of what my mother and maybe yours called "good manners." The Italians may have hung onto that archaic idea longer than it seems that we have.

The other side of the coin

As individuals, not even all Italians have mastered La Bella Figura. Service in stores all over Europe could derive a lot from Nordstrom or even Costco. Don't figure you can buy something and then return it without incredible hassle. In Italy sold is *sold*. And don't automatically expect idle store clerks to rush to wait on you. But if the merchandise, particularly jewelry, is costly, do expect them to follow you around like Inspector Clouseau.

Italians are also getting fatter like the rest of the world, particularly young women, maybe as many as 25% of them, according to my unscientific observations in Via Trinchese. Despite jiggling bellies, love handles and broader rear ends brought on by a newly acquired taste for fast foods, many of them still fancy skintight clothes that show them off at their worst. Young Italian guys don't seem afflicted to the same degree. Of course, in my case, bringing up this whole phenomenon is the pot calling the kettle black.

Road manners are another matter of cultural style. Italy is widely equated with wild driving. Yet I enjoy highway driving in Italy because highways are maintained in excellent condition and Italians simply do not dawdle. But to negotiate *city* driving you have to recognize that here it's offensive, not defensive driving, and follow the same unwritten, and sometimes very rude, rules. In cities, pedestrians leap for their lives. Things may be changing, but driving courtesy as we know it is about as rare as finding an armadillo in your bathtub—unless you're in Texas or Louisiana. It's also a recipe for getting rear-ended if you're driving

One thing is sure in Italy: You are going to eat better than you have ever eaten and you are going to be surrounded by the artifacts of one of the most astoundingly productive cultures the world has ever seen. And you don't have to go to Rome to do that; every corner of this country has glorious treasures.

Now that was actually two, three or four things, but, this is a place where emotions get you carried away—believe me, even though you can't see how I am waving my hands around in the air as I write.

Dick

Lecce, Italy

Poppies

An ancient amphitheater lies still half-buried under buildings in the heart of Lecce *antica*. In the sands of its arena, once soaked in blood, poppies have sprung up. We pass its silent mysteries on our evening *passeggiata*, joining throngs of Leccese in their traditional evening stroll through the city's streets.

The *anfiteatro* and its ruins are the first things you see when you walk into Piazza San Oronzo. Another is the old saint himself, standing atop a towering column that once marked the end of the Roman Appian Way. Oronzo's arm is raised in blessing to Lecce's inhabitants who cherish him as their patron saint. We've been coming this same way on many evenings for many years now.

Our usual destination is the Bar Cin Cin just a few

steps away from the amphitheater's time-ruined arches. This year we went there the evening after our arrival, looking forward to seeing the Cin Cin's owner, Gino Orlando. He'd owned the bar forever, knew everyone and everything, and was always happy to sit and talk with us. But this time Gino wasn't there and would never be again. His son told us he'd been taken away by a fatal heart attack in early June.

You should know about Italian neighborhood bars. They're not about Martinis, cabernet and Cosmos. The closest description I could come to is a cross between a coffee shop, a neighborhood pastry store, and an ice cream shop with beer, wine, liqueurs, and some little squares of focaccia with pizza sauce thrown in. They're not where people go to drink, they're where they go to sit and talk, meet their friends and watch the world go by.

When Gino's sons told us about their father, Adriana gasped and tears welled up in our eyes. Coming to Cin Cin on our first walk back in Lecce was like coming home to something constant. Like walking into your own front door after a long absence. Gino was supposed to be there, walking up to our table on the piazza with his warm smile and his hand outstretched as though it were only a day since we'd last been there, not a year.

His sons are trying to put things back together and carry on the business as a family. Over a glass of Prosecco we read the news article that Antonio brought outside to our table on the piazza from the bar. It told of his father as a man who had countless friends and made his mark with Leccese great and small. We met his wife, her eyes still swollen with these last weeks of grief. We read that Cin Cin had been the realization of a dream and we talked of a life that had been well lived.

We've come back to Cin Cin nearly every evening since that first night's walk. The life in the piazza is still the same. At eight, in the gently fading light of day, hundreds of swallows still create sudden aerial fireworks with startling explosions of flight twisting among the tops of the buildings and flashing into the sky and then are instantly, impossibly gone. Couples go by pushing strollers and baby carriages. Old men walk arm in arm. Girls vie to see who can wear the tightest clothes and teeter along on the highest heels. Old wives scold old husbands who walk with their hands clasped behind their backs thinking of Mussolini or rare stamps or cigars or forgotten dreams.

It is after all the people who matter. If the ancient

buildings surrounding the piazza, most of priceless and irreplaceable architecture, were ever to come down, we'd be unbelievably sorry. But losing someone you have enfolded into the embrace of your life is when you feel real pain and when tears come hot to your eyes.

    The consolation for me is to think of the poppies in the arena. Where life is lost, new life always starts. Lecce is said to be over 3,000 years old. It has been inhabited longer than Rome. That's a lot of poppies.

    "*Cin cin*" (say chin chin) *is a popular Italian toast. You can't find it in the dictionary and I have no idea where it came from or what it means. Adriana says it's Greek. But its spirit is clear — here's to you.*" Cin cin, Gino Orlando.

Dick

Lecce, Italy

Three cheers for the red, white and green

I was staring numbly into my coffee cup when Adriana came in from her morning shopping expedition. Her arms were laden with packages and she was beaming, "Look at what I got." I knew she'd been around the corner where Luigi Cataldo and Ninetto Catanzaro partner at their little fruit and produce store.

I could see the big watermelon peeking out of the bag, but she was just getting started. "Two pounds of beefsteak tomatoes too," she announced. Deeply red and ripe beauties. "Plus two pounds of cherry tomatoes, four cucumbers, a head of lettuce, parsley, arugula, and four red peppers—all for ten Euro. That'd cost twice as much at home," she proclaimed.

On top of that domestic coup she also hoisted a

dripping bag of several dozen shrimp and a shiny and still bright-eyed *orata*, an exquisite whitefish of great delicacy. Another 12 Euros. Again she thumbed her nose in the direction of our Seattle QFC and Metropolitan markets. La Regina dei Mari, the Queen of the Seas, a fine little fish store just around the other corner from us in Lecce is a part of her daily morning shopping route that might also include the pastry shop or a newsstand where she often picks up the morning paper.

The orata met its fate in a hurry, at lunch that same day. It was delicious. Now I have my sights set on a large chunk of that watermelon which is now icy cold in our refrigerator. *Anguria* as watermelon is called in Italian is a favorite here. Adriana has an aunt who insists it is really called *cocomero*, but that's Italy for you. Two Italians can make a boisterous disagreement about anything. Either way, Italians love it, maybe because it is the colors of the Italian flag—red, white and green.

My friend Juliet Shen back home would probably give them an argument about its nationality. She told me that in China watermelon is commonly prescribed for almost whatever ails you, from bad breath to dyspepsia. Eating watermelon is considered a vital factor in continued good health.

I have given this topic some purposeful pondering, to pin down why I like watermelon so much, considering that I am neither Chinese nor Italian. And I hate to start an international controversy, so please don't pass my comments along to anybody you know in either of those two countries. But the fact is they are simply misguided in their territorial claims.

I ask you to just stop and think: What is a watermelon? Try to see one, really *see* it in your mind's eye: Walk around the produce department and look at him lying there—*over there*, behind the bananas and in front of the spuds.

Compared to the kiwis and pears, he looks like a lineman for the Chicago Bears. Or, with those stripes, a big, green Tony the Tiger. Is it *rude* to be that big — or is a watermelon something special?

A watermelon may be more than you think.

If you were an ant marching around him in a field, you'd be walking around an amazing tank created solely for the storage of sunshine, connected to the rich, moist earth by a pipeline no human engineer could conjure.

To many a mother, the watermelon is that huge surprise lugged home in the bottom of a grocery bag. Worth struggling with, because look how those faces light up.

Despite the opinion of politicians and speech makers, the watermelon is the *real* guest of honor on the Fourth of July—and gets our full attention right up until they start the fireworks.

To those of us with artistic leanings a watermelon is an opportunity for sculpture with your fork, making tunnels and bridges. And finally an empty green boat when you've gotten every last drop of sweet, sweet juice.

The watermelon was in fact probably the culprit when your mother first said, "Will you please stop playing with your food?"

No doubt about it. The watermelon was Tom Sawyer's companion and a personal friend of Huckleberry Finn. It is paper plates, going barefoot, and learning the invaluable art of spitting seeds farther than anybody else.

To a little girl in a starched white dress it is one of the first challenges of being ladylike when you eat.

It is wiggling your toes in the cool, green grass and knowing that school is out and that being outside is in. It is a day at the lake, a ball game in the park, and the soft buzz of bees in the blossoms.

Icy cold from the creek, it beats any air conditioning ever invented. To say nothing at all of apples and oranges, which as you know you can't even compare to each other.

In the summer always carry a fork, so you're ready if you run into a watermelon someplace.

What is a watermelon? It is the Creator's announcement that the sun has come out. That nobody is looking if you get a little juice on your chin.

What is a watermelon? It is the best of tastes at the best of times. A slice of watermelon is the smile on the face of summer.

I can only look at a watermelon from my American perspective, to me it is more American than even apple pie. But I have to admit that both my heart and my taste buds tell me it is heaven's gift to *everyone*, particularly to those of us who are still at least partially stuck in childhood. And there must be others like me in Italy and China.

I have given this some serious thought, even though some may doubt my ability to do that. But I have been wondering if I could interest anybody at home in changing the colors of our flag.

Maybe just in the summertime.

Dick

Lecce, Italy
On the Fourth of July

Sempre dritto

There's no real need to tell you about Italian drivers. If you haven't heard about their mania for speed, you have only to look at a red Ferrari or a brutal Ducati road bike to see the idea captured in breathtaking two- or four-wheeled sculpture from Maranello or Bologna.

Volkswagen advertises "Drivers Wanted." BMW calls itself the "Driving Machine." These are lofty Germanic philosophical ideas connected with a kind of purism that doesn't exist in Italy. Italian driving is solely about getting there first.

The feel of the road, the crispness of the gearbox, the sheer aestheticism of mechanical precision matched to the demands of the highway have nothing to do with getting there first. The Italians do love German cars—simply because they get them there firster. If you're doing a paltry 160 kph (close to 100 mph), Italians in BMWs and Mercedes pass you like you're sitting at a rest stop eating a panino.

Getting there first is little hampered by traffic cops, speed limit warnings or roadside advisory signs. It is an inherent right of the Italian citizen and you see it displayed everywhere, not just on the road. Italians care much about *la bella figura*, dressing well, being well thought of, not being obtrusive or intrusive, and looking good. This concept of how one behaves and appears is undeniably important, but is trumped by the genetic need to get there first. Old ladies wedge themselves in ahead of you in supermarket lines and when you're waiting at the boarding gate of an airport. Well-dressed businessmen and responsible looking mothers with kids in the back seat make you leap for your life if you don't want to be run down in a crosswalk.

There is, in fact, no such thing as a line with people waiting in an orderly row. The queue, a perfectly straightforward notion built into English DNA, is missing in Italians. Instead there is a mob, ruled by the idea of getting there first. Painted cross walks are mere decoration, like gargoyle door knockers and sculpted angels on churches. Highway signs fall into much the same category. They seem to exist only to support a sign painting industry. While there are indeed traffic police and serious authorities responsible for public safety, they must either be mightily frustrated or are insiders in an astonishing national joke played on the rest of us.

This exclamatory street sign is a favorite of ours. We were talking about it with a house guest from the States, John Marrone. John is a law student with a natural curiosity about legal things. He suggested that the symbol apparently stood for WE REALLY MEAN IT and worked in conjunction with another warning of some sort. Sure enough, it's almost always close to another sign like this one warning of curves ahead, or one with a silhouette of a cow or a graphic of a bunch of bumps (or ocean waves—sometimes it's hard to tell.)

Getting there first is much more important than *where* you're getting to first. So Italian road signage has a kind of devil-may-care inexactness about it. A sign like this may either mean that you must turn left to go to Alberobello or could just as easily mean that Alberobello is *straight ahead!* Your choice. I usually opt for straight ahead because if you ask Italians for directions they invariably wave their arms in a variety of directions and then tell you *"sempre dritto."*

This is a spoken variation of the Turn Left or Go Straight Ahead sign. It literally means *straight ahead*, though in Italy there is hardly ever any straight ahead. Streets curve every which way, divide and suddenly peter out. No street ever has the same name for more than a few blocks, because The Powers That Be feel compelled to honor every dignitary, obscure saint, ancient military figure, local big shot, or major contributor with his own street name. It makes for messy maps, and many surprises, but then half the joy of driving here lies in getting lost. By always obediently steering *sempre dritto* we've discovered marvelous little towns, great cafes and wondrous sights we would have never seen if we had gone where we had intended.

Somehow the Italians survive their penchant for getting there first. I think it's not a demonstration of bravery or lack of fear, but actually a kind of cultural madness that overcomes them, like dancing the tarantella. Underneath the pedal-to-the-metal frenzy are a people who value security, conformity and safety. This is the only country where I've found bell pulls to summon help in public toilets. What help might be needed one can only imagine. But apparently the same Giovanni or Luigi or Francesca who practice driving like a blood sport seem to have some significant concern about falling off toilet seats. (Of course if there were a sign advising them to fasten their seatbelts, it would be ignored.) Maybe they could solve the problem with those toy steering wheels that little kids stick on daddy's dashboard.

Even parking practices reflect the Italian driver's need for speed. After all, there is no point in getting there ahead of everybody else if a whole bunch of other everybody elses have filled all the parking places. The immediate solution for that is double and even triple parking. A familiar curbside sight is a driver coming out of a store to discover that her parked car is blocked. It is the occasion for much screaming, arm waving, and fist shaking. The other option is to jam your car into any available space, no matter the size, no matter if you are halfway up on the sidewalk or completely across a crosswalk, and certainly no matter if you aren't parked in the same direction everybody else is. When it comes to parking styles, everybody in Italy is pro-choice. The point is to get in there somehow—*now*.

We hope you are finding your way through the summer safely. And by the way...

Dick
Lecce, Italy

"Eeww! What's this stuff?"

"Shut up and eat, dear."

I hate airlines.

Hi, we're in Italy. Getting from House A in Seattle to House B in Lecce took 26 hours door to door, including a five-hour wait in Rome for an Alitalia flight to Brindisi and a half hour home by car.

Home *here* seemed just like home there. The light switch in the kitchen was broken, the refrigerator wasn't refrigerating, somebody had appropriated our Scrabble game, and our son called to tell us his transmission was broken. ("Mom, help!")

In other words life is going on with us here just as it probably is with you there. Still, it's nice to be here. They like to say, "Getting there is half the fun." That may be true if you drive or ride a bike. Above is a picture from our trip.

We'd just been served "breakfast" on Delta Flight 1272, the first leg of our two-phase flight from Seattle to Rome. Its imminent arrival had been heralded by a spiffy four-color menu. From the pictures we could see that clearly this was not to be the old lukewarm scrambled eggs, a little wooden pork sausage, fake orange juice and dehydrated mini-roll that United, Alaska or Northwest had trotted out for years out of the goodness of their hearts. This was *upscale!* Something that would delight a Starbuck's patron—a cinnamon raisin bagel, cream cheese and strawberry jam. So it was also three dollars, not free.

Oh well, it sounded better than the alternative fruit plate I'd seen on the flight attendant's cart as he'd hustled down the aisle. That resembled high school cafeteria fruit salad, only in a miniaturized serving.

The vaunted bagel that arrived wasn't much better. It had been conveniently pre-dried out and came with a tiny cup of cream cheese and a hefty half teaspoon of rubbery strawberry jam artfully packaged in a little rectangle of plastic. What it didn't come with was anything to spread these delicacies on the bagel. It was far too calcified to eat plain. I grouched and muttered as Adriana patiently explained that knives were disallowed on airplanes these days. "Surely," I cried, "No self-respecting terrorist would try to overwhelm the air crew and hold passengers hostage with a dinky plastic knife."

"Shut up and dip little pieces of your bagel into the little bitty cream cheese thing, " she clarified. I should explain that Adriana is Catholic, which apparently has prepared her to submit to all kinds of outrageous abuse, like brutal nuns, self-flagellation, and other penances to atone for her various guilts. She only gets mad at the bank, but then their outrages are beyond normal endurance.

"To hell with dipping," I grumbled, attempting to spread cheese and strawberry goo on the bagel with my index finger. Fingers don't really work well for that purpose.

As Adriana and other passengers dipped I remembered that there was a nice heavy plastic bookmark in the paperback I'd tucked in the seat pocket in front of me. It worked fine as a spatula. And it was a new experience for me—the first time I've ever licked a bookmark before putting it back in my book. Now that airline passengers have all been effectively disarmed, I thought of how to sharpen it into a deadly weapon. As the signs say in the branch library, "Readers are Leaders." I knew my old army survival training would pay off.

We were then finally on the New York to Rome leg of our flight. We'd just polished off our Pot Roast dinner with Strawberry Cake. The main course was a spiritual experience. The Pot Roast was shreds of beef, about one ounce in all, the airline apparently having managed to duplicate Jesus' miracle of the loaves and fishes, feeding a whole planeload of passengers from a single five-pound roast. The dessert was a glop of artificial "whipping cream" spray-canned on top of some sort of strawberry mush, all epoxied onto what looked to be a decomposed Twinkie.

The night before last we had a bon voyage dinner with our friends the Palmers. Micki Jo served beautiful fresh strawberries ladled over delicious biscuit shortcake. The real thing like mama used to make. I've always loved strawberry shortcake. Tonight was the first time I've ever put it down after the first bite. But then what should you expect for only a couple of thousand dollars?

It also led me to the doorstep of my next writing project I envision to be a best seller—*The Airline Diet*. It's expensive, but weight loss is guaranteed. Just buy tickets that will take you anywhere for 14 days in a row. It doesn't matter where you go, so get the cheapest fares possible. Ask your travel agent to book flights that will keep you in the air continuously. *Eat only airline food.* You may buy food on board in addition to main meals, however you must choose only items that cost less than $2.00. This will limit you to water (tap), and maybe tea or coffee (generic.) You can even eat the little bags of free pretzels. A hundred of those wouldn't keep a parakeet alive.

I guarantee that you will lose 35 lbs.* or more in two weeks or you will be able to return my book for a full refund. Plus, you will become much more humble and compliant in the bargain. Where else can you get this much self-improvement in so short a time?

Let me off in Italy, please. Right by that restaurant at the bottom of the Spanish Steps.

Dick

Enroute over the Atlantic

On a British airline with British food you will lose much more.

> Stay right and continue two kilometers to Btfsplk.

"Lex" and other destinations

There is an old trick question: "Is the capitol of Louisiana pronounced New OR-lee-uns or New or-LEENS?" The answer, of course, is that it is pronounced *Baton Rouge*.

I hadn't yet recalled that grade school humor when last fall I sort of delicately suggested to Adriana that I might like to receive a GPS for Christmas. It was a subtle hint of course. I had merely cut a page out of an electronics catalog and marked exactly what I had in mind with a big circle of felt tip marker and left it where she keeps incoming bills on the kitchen counter.

Subtle as my hint was and despite that I had picked a pricey, top end model, and that we had both declared we were cutting down on Christmas expenses, I was surprised and delighted on Christmas Eve that Santa Adriana had granted my wish. She has amazing mind reading powers.

The GPS came into its own after we landed in Milan and needed to find our way to Bergamo the next day. In fact, it took on a life of its own as we strove to follow the directions spoken by its built-in guide, a female voice that accompanied the on-screen map provided by a satellite somewhere in the heavens. I came to think of the voice as "Lucille." Her personality was irritatingly evident. I pictured her as a sharp-edged and somewhat snappish New Yorker, skinny, impatient and probably smoking a cigarette.

Even in the downpour we drove into, Lucille did a pretty good job. Though I missed a couple of highway exits, she unfailingly got us back on the right track after announcing "Recalculating" in a tone that clearly sounded exasperated at my incompetence.

Our friends in a suburb of Bergamo had booked us into a hotel in nearby Stezzano. Lucille got us to the right street, and then apparently was in a hurry to run off for a potty break as she told us to turn left. We could barely see the road in the deluge of rain that overwhelmed our car's windshield wipers. Lucille returned to tell us we were at our destination at No. 43 Via Santuario. It turned out not to be a hotel, but a small restaurant, and *No. 44*. Next to it was the Catholic sanctuary the street was named after and nothing else on the country road that ran through mostly empty farm fields

Dutifully Adriana climbed out into the drenching rain and ran to the door of the inn, which was closed. We drove on but the numbers became bigger instead of smaller. On the way back, we stopped at the same inn, because Adriana now thought she had seen a light inside. She got out again and when she again slid back into the front seat her shoes and clothes were totally soaked and her hair was dripping wet, but she had proper directions. Lucille apparently never knew that No. 43 was one mile away from No. 44 and in the opposite direction. We got there without any further advice from our gal pal.

I have to say though that Lucille and the Garmin GPS were way better than any roadmap, and well worth what I paid for an extra memory card with detailed and almost miraculous maps of all the countries of Western Europe, right down to dinky towns I had never heard of.

But smart as Lucille is, or *thinks* she is, she is an ignoramus when it comes to pronouncing street names in a foreign language. Unfortunately, thoughtless foreigners have the extremely inconvenient habit of putting up street names in Italian, French, German, Spanish or Greek. Lucille can't deal with that and her pronunciation makes it impossible to coordinate what you are hearing with what is written on the signposts. For example, if you were driving around Seattle, would you recognize our home street, Ridge Drive Northeast, if a non-English speaking German or Italian advised to you to turn right at REED-jay DREE-vay Nort-ay-Ahst as he well might?

That's what Lucille does and her idea of Italian pronunciation is maddening. Later in our trip as we approached Rome's Leonardo da Vinci Airport at Fiumicino, she noted we should look for Ock-SIDDEN-tail. She turned out to be referring to Viale Occidentale, which the stupid Italians (and we) read aloud to ourselves as O-chee-den-TAHL-ay.

A bit ago we called a cab to take us to the far side of town here to pick up another rental car. With all the one-way streets I wasn't quite sure about the quickest route back to our home in Lecce, so I asked Adriana to stick Lucille in her purse for the drive home. Now you should know that around here Lecce is pronounced much like the Spanish word for milk—LATE-chay. Lucille got us back here but not without reassuring us that we had to "turn right on the superstrada (another verbal contortion) and continue to *Lex!*" "LATE-chay! LATE-chay!" we screamed in unison, both wondering if Mr. Garmin keeps Lucille on because they have something going on the side.

It's all part of the excitement of driving here and the whole experience is quite different than at home. At a current $9-plus per gallon to fill your tank with either *benzina* or *gasolio*, it is quite a bit more pricey.

Still the Italian road is devoted to a bravura style of driving with its own appeal after sitting behind some halfwit in the US who has stopped on a freeway on-ramp, afraid to merge until the nearest oncoming car is at least 500 yards away. In Italy they would simply be run over or honked off the highway by legitimately angry drivers.

Italian highways are designed for speed and so are driving customs. Unlike at home where every freeway lane is jammed full, inside lanes in Italy are intended for passing only. Drivers who want to pass you turn on their left turn signals or flash their headlights to let you know when they wish to pass. Then as soon as they are past you, they almost immediately cut back in front of you (without signaling) and leave the passing lane free, sometimes missing your front fender by a whisker. It's all part of demonstrating their flair as drivers and their Italian passion to *get there*.

All over Italy principal highways are straddled by ubiquitous Autogrills that stretch overhead from one side of the road to another and at either end feature major brand gas stations, convenience stores, and informal restaurants serving hot and cold food.

Well, sometimes hot and cold. They often seem to get the two ideas confused. We stopped in one Autogrill for lunch —veal cutlet, vegetables, a roll and some mini bottles of wine. The roll was cold. The meat and vegetables were more luke than warm, and the wine was about like a pop starlet's IQ—

room temperature. It also cost us much more than a far better lunch in even a fine restaurant anywhere else around here.

One lifesaving feature of the Autogrill though is its ample and well-kept bathrooms. As in many public places here, they have an attendant at the door and it is customary to leave her a tip. It used to be a few lire, maybe worth a quarter. Now it seems like most of the smallest coins you get are one Euro.

Pre-Euro coin discovered in ancient Roman pay toilet.

Adriana and I each made use of the facilities after we'd had lunch. The attendants collected a Euro apiece to stick in their apron pockets. At prevailing exchange rates that was about $3.10 to pee.

Like they used to say about yachts though, if you have to ask the price, you can't afford it.

Ciao! Yours for economy travel—(that's CHOW, not ki-AY-oh, Lucille.)

Dick

Lecce, Italy

Today the cherries came in

These aren't ordinary sweet cherries. We've already bought some of those. These are *ciliegie ferrovie*, a deeply sweet, dark cherry that everybody here waits for.

Three or four weeks ago Adriana asked about them at the produce store down the block and around the corner from our place. It's a dumpy little place run by Luigi Cataldo and his partner Ninetto Catanzaro. Outside their sign just says *"Frutta,"* fruit. Inside are every kind of astonishingly delicious fruit and vegetable available here. Also the kind of personal service the rest of the world has sadly outgrown. Ciliegie ferrovie ("railroad cherries" for a reason no one can remember) are only harvested for a couple of weeks, and they have a flavor that makes your tongue sing and dance...

(Okay, I'm back, I just got up to grab a handful.)

When Adriana asked when they'd be available, Luigi looked at her as if she should have known and said, "*Allora*, June 10, Signora!" Of course, we should have known. It was like the scheduled arrival of a friend coming to stay a few weeks.

Food here is not simply something to eat, but a work of love, an occasion, and a principal topic of conversation whether it's presented at home or in a restaurant. Most Italian food is great because Italians care about it so much, but also because the ingredients are usually far better than we're used to at home. The fruit and vegetables aren't always cosmetically beautiful and don't look like they've been stamped out of a mold, but their quality and flavor are sensational.

At Frutta, which is slightly smaller than our living room and piled high with crates, Luigi and Ninetto bring in nearly everything fresh from local farms every morning, sometimes still warm from the sun and the lingering heat of the fields. When we go home and once again eat tasteless BC Hothouse tomatoes for $3 a pound, we will weep. L&N load Adriana down with bags of cherries, oranges, zucchini, arugula, lettuce, peaches, potatoes, green beans and watermelon, as much as she can carry for maybe 25 dollars. And either of the two partners would carry it home for her if she let them.

We've had our last run of company here, so we're finally retrenching on eating out. My cousin from

Germany and her husband left just yesterday. Charlie Barnett, my friend and colleague from Fox Island, Washington left the day they arrived. Before that we enjoyed our first week here with Dan and Pat Brotherton, from Bainbridge Island.

With each of them we toured a lot of sights and sampled a lot of great wines and food in our favorite places. Just on Monday, we were once again in Alberobello, a hill town filled with *trulli*, strange cone-shaped houses of uncertain origin. We'd been there a bit over a week ago too, with Charlie, and waited out a thunderstorm and downpour in Ristorante L'Aratro (The Plow), which is in several trulli that have been joined together. We'd go back there just for their focaccia. I was also supposed to say hello to the waitress for Charlie who'd fallen instantly in love with her, but she wasn't there. Sorry, Charlie. Domenico, the owner, was, however, and after a long, long lunch he took us up the street to another restaurant he owned and bought us each a glass of *limoncello* while we sat under an umbrella and looked out over the white, sun-kissed buildings. We wish you could have been there, too.

Both of us are frazzled from translating. We're now hoping to concentrate on our Italian. Adriana speaks it exceedingly well, since she teaches it back home at the University of Washington and I do okay. But with Pat, Dan, Charlie, Uwe and Annemarie we had a Tower of Babel going in English, Italian, German and a little left-over French to fill in the bare spots. I speak German well, but realized that I was somehow stirring Italian words into German sentences. It's a stew recipe that doesn't really work. We still had a ball with everybody and hope that the dictionaries of Germany and Italy forgive us.

A couple of pictures illustrate the vast sweep of the Italian experience:

The one above is a slice of the delicious beach at Torre dell'Orso, near here on the Adriatic. I took the other one in the cathedral of Otranto, south of Torre dell'Orso. A little history is in order before you look at that latter picture. This part of Italy, like much of southern Europe was invaded by the Muslim Turks in the 15th and 16th Centuries. Along the Adriatic coast stone watch towers were erected to alert inhabitants about imminent terror. A system of signal fires provided an early warning, blazing the message from tower to tower.

Torre dell'Orso, "the tower of the bear," overlooked one of the likely landing sites. On July 12, 1480 raiders from as many as 200 Turkish ships overwhelmed the defenses of nearby Otranto. Bishop Stephen Pendinelli and the garrison commander, count Francesco Largo, were sawed in two, alive. Local Christians were told to become Muslims or die. Hundreds refused. Their tongues were cut out and then their heads were cut off.

Behind the figures of Mary and Jesus in the cathedral, glass-fronted cabinets that at a distance appear to be gray tapestries, hold the skulls of 800 men, women and children who died for their Christian belief. Behind a panel in the same room, a series of drawers contain hundreds of preserved tongues that still speak of their faith. The Muslims conquered southern Europe well up into France, until German princes and the King of Poland finally drove them out at the gates of Vienna in 1683.

Unfortunately they're still at it. In France, Spain, Chechnya, England, Somalia, Thailand, China, the Philippines and maybe 30 or 40 other places. Time to call the Poles?

We hope you are fine and keeping your head. Best from Adriana and me. Ciao.

Dick

Lecce, Italy

"Never try to teach a pig to sing, it wastes your time and annoys the pig."

La botola
Don't take a whoopee cushion to a gunfight

We got hooked. Italian television can be pretty bizarre, but *La botola*, a sort of Italian Idol, drew us in. We've only admitted watching it to a few very close friends.

A couple of years ago, we got similarly entranced by another Italian show called *Sposami*. Its premise differed entirely from La botola's amateur talent format. Instead of performers it featured couples who had been engaged and/or living together for years, while one of the pair had been longing for marriage that never happened. Some even had kids. Their patience was wearing thin.

One of the contestants, usually some guy who managed to put off popping The Question with endless excuses, is invited to the show under false pretenses. He usually expects it to be for a feature story interview or some other kind of game show. His gal pal is tucked away behind the scenery when he is led onstage. She pops out in full bridal regalia (courtesy of the show) and confronts him to declare her love and demand "*sposami!*" (marry me!)

The guy has only a few minutes to decide. At stake are a diamond wedding ring set, expensive clothes, and an exotic honeymoon cruise. He is allowed to call his mom, his best friend or his favorite advisor and then he has to face his lady. More than once, the answer has been something like, "Hell, no." Once a woman declared, "How dare you do this, you *bleep*," and stalked off the stage.

The hopes, the doubt, the tears were real. American TV is in love with "reality" shows, but the outcomes seem more like fairy tales. This is more like life itself than theater.

La botola is in the same mold.

The audience is the judge and contestants are introduced usually by a mother, a sibling, or a best friend. They come out individually to sing, dance, do magic tricks, or perform acrobatics. One notable contestant demonstrated how he could hypnotize a chicken. After they perform they are brought out on the stage in pairs where they stand about ten feet apart as the MC reminds the audience of their performance. As they are being electronically scored by the audience, the MC walks over to a large lever with a red handle and yanks it. Long seconds tick by.

The camera pans back and forth from one to another. Suddenly, the loser plunges through a concealed trap door into a large tank of water under the stage where he or she has to swim out and escape, helped by a friendly stagehand.

Life itself tends to work that way, and here Italian television is much more accurate than its American cousin. Despite nasty Simon Cowell, runners up on American Idol are lavished with praise. So are the sort-of celebrities who fail to win first place on Dancing With The Stars. In Italy they go in the tank or go home crying. You only win by not losing.

Former Border Patrolman and ex-Marine Bill Jordan survived countless gun fights. His talent was his ability to draw his revolver, fire and hit his target in .27 seconds. He came to work prepared, had the right equipment, and was armed with the knowledge of a certain uncomfortable truth—there is *no second place winner*. That's not only the title of the book he wrote about gun fighting, it's worth thinking about.

Our popular culture seems determined to make everybody feel happy as an entitlement. Even obnoxious losers rejected by Donald Trump keep returning to fame and fortune on follow-up shows.

On La botola a beautiful, conservatory-trained operatic soprano in a lovely dress went in the tank in favor of a homely guy who sang a pretty good version of Granada. He hit the mark, she didn't, despite a stunning performance on her part. I loved her, the audience didn't. They got to call the shots. And there were no shots of her being fished out in her ruined dress for a consolation interview. La botola by the way means "The Trapdoor."

Life is beautiful. It's also unfair and both of those ideas take some getting used to. I have a hunch that Italians, with 3,000 years of glory, wars, plague, and culture behind them, have more experience with that reality than we do. Otherwise we wouldn't be patting school kids on the head and beaming, "Good job!" when they multiply 3 times 21 and get 43, but they sure tried hard.

We also wouldn't be sticking them in soccer matches where nobody keeps score because it doesn't feel good to get beaten.

Of course, it doesn't feel good to get beaten, that's why most successful people don't allow it to happen to themselves. It strikes me as inane to start telling kids otherwise, when sooner or later they are going to be standing on a trapdoor where they discover reality. You ought to get ready for it as soon as possible.

Our stupid celebrity worshipping culture isn't big on preparing us for reality. Movie stars who spawn children with whomever is handy aren't very good role models. Neither are all the ex-con "athletes" who rape, loot and pillage as after-work recreation, or business people using insider information to defraud stock-owning families, or clerics with their hands in little kids' pants, or city councilmen lining their pockets with "donations." They all get away with it far too long before somebody pulls the lever on the trapdoor.

I suspect most of us ultimately learn more by going in the tank a time or two, or three, than we do by our successes. When I was a little kid, I played with my mother's hairpins, going "Rrrrr. Rrrrrr," sticking them in an electric wall outlet pretending I was starting my car. It was a startling experience, but I still did it a *second* time before my brain kicked in. Fortunately my mom wasn't on the scene either time to pat me on the head and declare, "Good job, sweetheart."

Now I have an exciting new position as a Grandpa. Grandpas, according to prevailing mythology, have all kinds of wisdom. So I have been thinking hard and hoping to come up with some nuggets I can pass along to our granddaughter. I think I will tell her about La botola. I may even tell her about my "car keys," although I never even told my mother about that.

Dick

Lecce, Italy

The moon is full

The Italians are acting strangely today. Perhaps they are only being Italian and I am making more of this than is warranted. But this is a superstitious country where certain dishes must be stirred only clockwise, where Fridays are a dangerous day to make decisions, and where many men and women wear little serpent-like charms resembling sperm to ward off the "evil eye."

Still, it has been scientifically established that the gravitational pull of the moon influences both the tides and the behavior of a variety of living creatures. Published solunar tables accurately guide fishermen and hunters to the feeding, sheltering and sleep patterns of both fish and birds. Even our word "lunatic" refers to deviant behavior wrought by the pull of the moon.

Combine that irresistible tug with one of the world's more emotional peoples and things just happen. One of them is a change in traffic patterns in a country where "driving order" is a vastly overstated description of how things work.

I didn't realize what was going on on the day of the first full moon. I couldn't see it since it was daytime, but it was clear that overnight hundreds of drivers had somehow been replaced by alien life forms determined to kill me. Italians tend to be scofflaws anyway, blithely running red lights and double parking on streets barely wide enough for legal parking. But suddenly entire blocks were jammed end to end with double parked cars for their entire length, not just one or two.

All over scores of drivers entered intersections at full speed with glazed, unseeing eyes like movie zombies, while the few remaining unpossessed drivers stood on their brakes to avoid calamity. At numerous traffic circles or "roundabouts," careening drivers formed an impenetrable race track, that you could only enter by closing your eyes and reciting a prayer. Parking places became non-existent. People squeezed head-on into spaces left between parallel parked cars. Every crosswalk had a parked car blocking it or an interlocking row of scooters and motorcycles with no room for pedestrians to squeeze through.

And then the night came and the full moon shone. It provided new cosmic light and inspiration for the graffiti artists who apparently hang someplace like bats or Count Dracula, only to emerge at night and cover benches, shop walls, marble monuments, gorgeous churches and palaces, and almost every sign, pillar, post and passageway with their hideous and despicable expressions of malcontent and mental disorder that mars the face of this otherwise beautiful city and many others.

"I hate everybody"

In some towns equally demented mayors have decided that these artists should have a dedicated space to express themselves and have taxed the overburdened citizenry to provide it. But when the whole world is your canvas, who needs it? The tide of visual filth rolls on in tsunami proportions, clearly assisted by the tug on feeble intellects exerted by our pal the moon.

Spray paint isn't the only medium favored for expressing the bold vision of moonstruck morons. T-shirts are also a grand canvas. And for those of you who go around proclaiming that George Bush single-handedly turned Europe anti-American, you have to wonder why they love all those T-shirts with "American" phrases on them, names of fake sports teams, or words strung together that make absolutely no sense. It seems it doesn't make any difference as long as it is in English and looks American. It is also quite clear that some of the folks who wear them know no English and understand nothing of what they say. A couple of years ago my hair stood on end to see an over-endowed 15-year old wearing a shirt that proclaimed what she was willing to do on a first date. If her father had known what it said, I think she wouldn't have made it out of the house, and perhaps not alive.

As the moon waxed full here, it also became hotter as the *scirocco* winds swept up from Africa bearing its sickly, sweaty humidity. In Switzerland a similar wind called the *Föhn* has been blamed for a marked periodic increase in suicides. Mother Nature simply doesn't seem to care that she drives some of her more vulnerable children nutty.

At the height of the full moon we drove across the peninsula to Porto Cesareo, a seaside town on the Ionian Sea. As we drove through the countryside we noticed two things, first that there was little or no graffiti on farm field walls or the buildings of small towns. The second was that the wind was shifting from a scirocco to the *tramontana* wind that blows from the north. Blessedly, the temperature started to drop.

We checked into a fine hotel, the Hotel Falli that overlooks the boardwalk and Porto Cesareo's busy fishing fleet. A four-star place, it came with air-conditioning, one of mankind's greatest inventions, and a superb restaurant where we had a sumptuous lunch. There was no graffiti on the hotel and none on the hotels on either side of the Falli. Yet while Falli is the name of the two brothers who own the hotel, the mere mention of it later to friends brought sudden snorts of mirth to friends, apparently evoking an Italian slang term involving, shall we say, phallic activities. Maybe it was graffiti after all.

That evening we strolled the boardwalk along the sea and finally stopped at a portable stand selling fresh peeled almonds, licorice, and all kinds of sweets and candies. Adriana who loves me so much that she occasionally lets me indulge in something that is unhealthily delicious bought me a bag of *croccante,* a joyously crunchy peanut brittle style candy made instead with large and lovely white almonds.

I bit down and immediately pulled a crown off one of my teeth.

I looked up and the moon was still full. We fled for our hotel and parked ourselves outside next door at a pizza place where I had a beer and gingerly gnawed on a memorably good pizza. We leaned back to watch the passing parade of meandering bicyclists, old fisherman arguing politics, strolling lovers, and families. Despite the moon and the $1,000 tooth that was now in my pocket, I still felt safe and like things were getting more or less back to normal. We both watched a young family approach us, a mom, dad and a child. "What a nice family," Adriana remarked. "Did you see the father's T-shirt? " I asked. *"It said, 'F___ the Queen!'"*

I'm not sure what the Queen had done to inspire that. I am not even sure which queen it was about, there aren't many left around. Maybe it was an English tourist with a legitimate gripe.

More likely it was the moon.

Before we left home for Italy we had watched one of our favorite movies, Moonstruck. I didn't realize there was so much more to it than I'd thought.

To this recommendation painted on a wall in Bergamo I can only add, "Stay indoors when the moon is full. At least around here."

Dick

Lecce, Italy

Men are Vespas, women are Valentines

For a long time now, I have thought that reader boards at retail establishments contained some of the most profound insights into the human condition.

Near our house in Seattle a public-spirited dry cleaner often showcases brilliant and useful observations like: *Almost anything is easier to get into than to get out of.* At the other end of town a food importer finally explained one of the basic laws of the physical universe in a way we can all understand: *A day without sunshine is like, well, night.* Like a lot of great discoveries, many of these staggering truths were set forth despite severe obstacles—like having to use upside down 3s or Ws, because they'd run out of Es or Ms.

For years I admired those who had ferreted out these verities and openly wondered how they did it. Then I looked in our dishwasher and realized that valuable insights are often right under your nose. There, waiting for the rest of the rack to fill up with soiled dishes, wine stained glasses, and knives and forks messy with the remains of last night's dinner, were cups from this morning's coffee. Mine, a treasured mug with a picture of a Vespa scooter on it. The other, Adriana's tall cup covered with pink and red hearts—a gift she'd given herself.

The contrast triggered a sudden flash of realization. "My God, she's different." Or maybe it was, "My God, *I'm* different." I rushed to the cupboard to confirm my new theory and there it was: My other two favorite cups were side by side—my "I heart my dog's head" cup and my imposing and presidential Ronald Reagan cup. Her cups all seemed to have designs involving butterflies, cups I couldn't bring myself to use unless mine were all in the dishwasher.

Clearly, the butterfly theme was something I couldn't readily identify with. It's obviously some kind of feminine cult symbol. Maybe it has something to do with life stages. The old cup that Adriana replaced with the Valentine one, was decorated with dozens of rabbits making love, if that term can be used for the rabbit version of procreation. I think she had it since she was about 25 years younger. I always wondered, but never asked,who gave it to her.

The same day I discovered the Vespa/Valentine Theory, I found a shopping list not three feet away: "Baby diapers," it said. And, mysteriously, "Butterflies." Not six hours later my bride was showing me a dangly, hovering butterfly thing that was supposed to keep Our Divine Granddaughter happy in her upstairs crib-away-from-home.

So far, we've been through baby showers, Christmas and a First Birthday where butterflies figured heavily. Rabbits probably come later at the kid's bridal shower, which I think is probably also in the planning stages. There is much female snickering and goings-on about sex and panties at these later stage, pre-wedding events.

One thing that characterizes both of these life-stage markers is a feminine form of welfare called "registering." This means taking advantage of an apparently God-given female right to ask for and expect to receive a whole treasure trove of expensive gifts.

This is a demonstration of chutzpah no guy I know would ever dream of. It was invented by a conspiracy of Macy's, Nordstrom, various appliance makers and Hallmark. Now, if you are a girl, you apparently can "register" for all kinds of happenings —from your *First Bra* to your *Sweet Sixteen Party* to

Getting Engaged to all the usual other events that are a ticket to valuable merchandise. Of course, in today's advanced world of ever-earlier "adulthood" these events can even happen in an entirely different order than I have listed.

I'd never heard of "registering" until I mentioned to a copywriter friend years back that I was getting married. He sent out a notice to everybody at McCann-Erickson where we worked that I was getting married and was registered at Warshal's, a local sporting goods store. "Dick's pattern," he told them, "is Smith & Wesson." Nobody gave me a thing. It doesn't work that way for us.

One exception: I did of course register for the draft. That worked fine and I was in the Army before I knew it. I did get a pair of combat boots and a free set of clothes out of it, all a kind of unlovely, drab color. Unfortunately, for the next two years all of my choices were extremely limited and often accompanied by "Request Denied."

Despite their apparently unfair entitlements and expectations that are grasped only by reading tea leaves in the bottom of your Harley Davidson or Boston Red Sox mug, women are noble creatures, much to be admired and even worshipped, when you've found the right one.

Their emotional computers though are as different from ours as a Mac is from a PC. And they don't come with instruction books. You just have to *guess* and trying to fathom hours of scowling silence by simple *asking*, "What's the matter, dear?" won't help because the answer is always, "Nothing!" uttered with clearly malevolent intent.

Some of the world's best male minds have struggled how nothing can apparently be something—and how it seems to be incumbent on them to figure out what it is. My friend Val thought he'd found a guidebook when his wife finished reading a popular book on the differences between men and women. She urged him to read it because she said it described him and his shortcomings to a T. Always willing to learn something important, Val was baffled to discover that it described *her* to a T, but didn't seem to say anything he recognized about himself at all.

I think they had a fight about it.

Later, his daughter who was trying to be helpful explained that some of her mother's stresses came from Val's freelance design career and its irregular paychecks. "She is insecure," the girl explained.

"Insecure?" Val gasped. "We've been married for decades. In all that time, why didn't she just say, *"Honey, I'm insecure?* It would have taken just two words. Isn't that what words are for?" Poor hopelessly hopeful Val.

Val is a Vespa. I'm writing this from our home in Italy and I can hear Vespas and motorcycles tearing along Via Zanardelli just beneath our terrace. Vespas make quite a bit of noise. Women are Valentines and tend to speak the wispy sign language of butterflies.

It has its own dictionary and that isn't sold in bookstores.

But it doesn't matter, because even if you somehow managed to find a copy of it, you'd quickly learn that the definitions are changed every day.

Dick

Lecce, Italy

If you try to fail, and succeed, which have you done?

Dutch 1985–1997

I took Dutch to Willapa Bay today and buried him beneath an ancient tree on a hillside dancing with dandelions.

How different it was from our many other travels to our favorite place. Those times before he'd always wake up from his pre-dawn doze while we were still miles from our destination. He'd press his nose to the car window, catching in some mystical way the far-off scent of cattails and tidal waters, of ducks and the tasks he was born for. But this morning there was no waking up. Just hours before, as I held him in my arms, he slipped the leash of life, finally escaping a lingering illness.

Dutch shared my life, as I shared his, while a dozen years flew by. He made friends for us at home and with the dogs and men who walked the fields with us. From puppyhood on he was my constant companion in the agency where I worked and later in my own office. He was a bridge to a new marriage and a new family and a perfect ambassador through all of it. These relations were a tribute to a great, kind heart, but not his true work.

You may own a dog like Dutch (and I hope you do), but you won't know all of what he is about until you share a misty morning when rosy whispers of dawn barely hint at distant hills, black on black, and the wings of invisible birds whistle in the still gathered darkness. Then, if you touch him with your hand, you'll sense the same shiver of excitement that stirred an ancestral wolf pack. You'll see eyes filled with flame that see the unseen. And you'll feel a heart beat of pure joy, and realize it's yours joined with his.

As I write this, my eyes are filled with tears and a terrible ache has seized my heart. But I can still see Dutch, now in an endless green field, running, running, running far ahead to catch a scent of heaven.

He pauses to look back at me, "C'mon slowpoke, catch up!" He knows that my legs aren't what they used to be either. He's out of sight just now, but I know my dog. Just over the next rise, at the water's edge, he and the game are waiting.

Someone once said that dogs are filled with joy because their god walks among them. It is really the other way around.

Dick

South Bend, Washington

> "We are alone, absolutely alone on this chance planet: and, amid all the forms of life that surround us, not one, excepting the dog has made an alliance with us."
> —Maurice Maeterlinck

It's a dog's life

If you've read about Dutch in my postcards, you've probably got me figured for a dog guy. Or perhaps it might be because I've given you a lift in my old hunting van, which is permanently saturated with the scent of Eau de Lab and seems to be upholstered in dog hair.

I've given up apologizing for the car, since every trip takes me back to another time and place in memory like a rusty, rattling time machine.

From the beginning there have been dogs in my life, except for one dogless stretch in my Army and married life, both of which started about the same time. I was going to say "dog-free," but that makes it sound like having a mutt around is a worthless habit that one should kick—*"we sprayed the entire house, so we are finally dog-free."*

From my earliest glimmerings of memory my family consisted of Mama, Papa, Freddy, Diane, Peggy & Schnappsy. Freddy was my older brother Fred, Diane my sister. Peggy was a black and white fox terrier. Schnappsy was her offspring and product of a liaison between Peggy and an amorous dachshund, a mysterious and unknown suitor, who appeared from and disappeared into nowhere. I can still imagine him twisting the tips of the evil looking pencil-thin mustache on his upper lip.

Schnappsy's basically white body mirrored the black patches of his mother's. But the rest was pure dachshund, a breed bred to hunt badgers. He became my brother's personal property and together they hunted the woods that then blanketed Seattle's rural areas north of the city limits where the pavement ended and dirt roads began. I can still see my brother with his .22 striding for his personal hunting grounds or the rat infested dump, with Schnappsy's stumpy legs a blur as he raced ahead to catch a scent of their prey.

I don't remember what happened to Peggy, but Schnappsy suddenly disappeared and my brother spent tearful days walking through the woods, down country roads and going from isolated house to house calling his name. He found him near home, drowned in a abandoned well. My brother brought his sodden body home and we buried him in the yard and our hearts felt pain I had never felt.

We had lots of other animals that came and went.

Dozens of chickens, pigeons, ducks, a cow and calves, an obnoxious goat, and a couple of turkeys. And cats that appeared from nowhere. My father who prowled the woods to pick wild blackberries in patches he kept secret found a whole sack full of kittens at the end of a dead end road into the woods where city people drove to dump their trash. Covered with hundreds of fleas, they were lucky to have escaped being thrown at night into nearby Haller Lake. My parents bathed them and gave most of them away. We kept one or two, but in that era nobody counted cats and they were always transferred to my sister, Diane, as her charges. Every so often they would disappear only to be replaced by strays that came from nowhere, but who always found a saucer of milk at our place. To most of us, except my sister, they were cats, not pets.

Lumpy was Fred's next dog. A happy, active liver and white Springer Spaniel who'd come from a line of hunters, just my brother's cup of tea. Lumpy was with us until I was almost out of high school, a wonderful companion who had the unfortunate habit of also hunting neighbor's chickens. He disappeared twice. We found him both times, a day or so later, hiding in our basement in a pool of blood. Once shot through from shoulder to shoulder with a rifle bullet, once cut down by a shot gun with a mass of pellets in his body.

He brought a mighty terror into our house as we fought to save his life. With tears, prayers, and a good vet he lived to a ripe old age. To my sister and me he was like a sibling. When Fred went into the Army toward the end of WWII, I felt the same fears for him as I felt for Lumpy as he lay wounded. Fred came home safe to us, and to Lumpy who was still there to lick his face as we kissed our brother.

Those were dogs of my childhood and, as much as I loved them, the past inevitably grows a little dimmer with every year and they are no longer as vivid in my memory as those that came later. Tino, a ferocious miniature poodle that I bought for my late wife. I recklessly taught him bad habits, like how to snarl and lunge when I said, "Tino, you are a *Doberman!*" My friend Harry Watkins broke his finger trying to escape from Tino's attack when he had called him a "sissy dog" and we were compelled to prove he was bigger inside than outside.

Later he was followed by Candy, a very ladylike black Standard Poodle who became my duck hunting dog, an occupation this beautiful breed was originally bred for—not rhinestone collars and absurd haircuts.

When she was a more mature lady, I decided I needed a hunting dog that did not stick its paw in the water first to decide whether it was warm enough to swim after a downed duck in a muddy pond. Actually, I didn't decide that at all. I had been widowed, Candy was aging and I felt alone. But that was before I spied a handwritten sign in the supermarket with a phone number and "Chocolate

Lab Puppies For Sale." The address was nearby—the Murphy's.

"We have only one left," Murphy told me. "If we don't sell him, we'll donate him to St. Monica's auction. "Oh, I just like to look at puppies," I said. "I have a dog, I don't want to buy one."

"Then just take him home tonight and play with him, you can bring him back in the morning," he fiendishly offered. That was Dutch and he never went back to the Murphy's again, except to visit his mother. He was at my side at home and at work for the next 12 years.

When he was old, I thought he needed an intern, somebody he could teach the duck hunting ropes to. Enter Ben. Like Dutch a Chocolate Lab, but with eyes so beautiful we laughingly called him "Maybelline." He would be my constant companion until just last December, the two dogs granting me 25 long years of tail-wagging chocolate love and joy.

Today we still have Buddy, the Cocker Spaniel I gave Adriana for Christmas over a dozen years ago. I bought him some weeks before the holidays but didn't bring him home until Christmas Eve. While he was still in exile in a pet shop I visited him every day to carry him outside where he could get used to cars, passersby and the world. And I told him not to worry, he'd have it made in his new life that lay ahead. Now an old gentleman, quite deaf, and slow to get up, most of that life sadly lies behind him. I know that all too well from sharing dogs' lives that seemed to pass far too quickly.

The end of each of those lives brought an aching heart. Yet each had given me something unique and priceless. If you have owned a dog or if one has owned you, you know what I am talking about.

Somebody wrote "A dog has one aim in life—to bestow his heart." So if you have loved and lost a dog, please remember that gift. In giving it, the dog says, "I am leaving now. Please take care of this for me."

Your heavy heart feels the way it does because your dog has left it stuffed so full with love.

Dick

Seattle, Washington

The intern

Ben is gone. He died in my arms early this morning. He didn't quite make it to Christmas to sit once again excitedly looking up at his Christmas stocking on the bookcase. And he fell a bit short of his 13th birthday, still two months off.

He wasn't short of anything else however, even though for too long I stupidly thought he was. When Ben came to live with us, though I loved him, he joined another dog who had a grip on my heart. Ben had a lot to compete with and he was only a little fuzzy bundle of chocolate brown fur and big feet.

Because I had Dutch, a wonderful dog, I hadn't really given any thought to another dog. But, like most people I know, I am a sucker for puppies. When I heard that some folks wanted to donate a Chocolate

Lab pup to our church auction, I told Adriana, "Honey, I am going to drive down to Maple Valley to check out that donated dog and make sure it is a good one."

"You're going to come home with a puppy," she said. "No, I'm not. No puppy. No way," I replied indignantly. *How could she think that?*

It was a nice Spring weekend and a pleasant drive. There were ten little dogs in the litter. All boys. Eight weeks old and full of ferocious life, they were tumbling over each other shredding plants and shrubs in the owners' back yard. They looked so much alike that I stuck little pieces of duct tape on their heads with numbers to tell them apart.

The one for the church looked great. But before I left, another one somehow unlocked my car and sneaked inside. Of course I didn't notice him sitting on my lap until I was almost home. By then it was too late.

Sweet Chocolate Ben. That was his kennel name. We called him Ben, after a book of doggy cartoons starring a goofy dog of the same name. Dutch looked at him, sniffed him, seemed to say he was okay and walked off.

I had spent many hours training Dutch and he was a serious duck hunter, much admired and envied by my hunting companions. When Ben got old enough he came along with us, without most of the training I'd lavished on his older "brother." But he watched Dutch and somehow he caught on. In a while the intern was a rival of the master. Yet I kept on making unfavorable comparisons, relegating Ben to a back seat in my favor.

It was not until Dutch was gone and Ben was two years old that I finally really saw him. And saw how blind I'd been. Ben, Sweet Chocolate Ben, loved me beyond all reason. He lived up to his name, the soul of sweetness. My constant companion, he shared my office until my office and Ben both came home early this year. He won over everybody he met and he took a place in my heart as no dog has before. We had years and years of soft, sweet joy together.

This morning with my hand on his chest I felt his own great heart slow, tremble and finally stop beating after months of old age wear and many recent days of infirmity. I kissed his head and closed his eyes and wished that I had loved him even harder.

Dick

Seattle, Washington

Pancake makeup

There are a lot of things I just don't notice. Unfortunately, many of them are things like not noticing that Adriana has a new haircut, which for some reason I am supposed to comment on. I'm sure I would notice sudden and total baldness, but a few millimeters off the ends of her hair?

When I was a kid in school, one of the girls had a large port wine stain on her face. I may have *seen* that, but I really didn't notice. What I did notice was that suddenly one day it *vanished*. Now there *was* something. It took my mother to tell me it was pancake makeup. Har. Har. What a funny idea. Where's the syrup? Nudge. Nudge.

For years I gave no further thought to this strange stuff until one afternoon I followed my wife through the cosmetics department of our local Macy's.

Women were perched on stools getting makeovers, contorting their faces while cosmeticians applied rare and universally expensive potions to their faces. Then there were the cosmeticians themselves. Their complexions were totally perfect—in fact *plasticized*. Their pores were gone, replaced by an impermeable coating that looked like a flesh-colored version of the Bondo I'd used to repair a dented fender back when I still did that kind of thing. Pancake makeup! The second time I'd actually noticed it.

The third time was under far less stylish circumstances and involved the first known application of pancake makeup by dumb animals. It was not a result of an evolutionary awakening like sign language being used by chimpanzees.

It happened only because our local Metropolitan Market was barbecuing Kobe beef burgers outside their entrance with a little cafe set up next to their parking lot.

We'd stopped there to pick up a few things on our way to our cabin at Willapa Bay. The sizzling burgers smelled so good we paused to eat there, leaving our dogs in the car with all our weekend stuff.

We had food in the car but took care to cover it up, because Buddy, our Cocker Spaniel, was endlessly and notoriously hungry. Once Adriana had put a packet of freshly made, uncooked pasta in the back of her car and one of those two foot long baguettes of French bread. She stopped somewhere for a minute or two and Buddy ate the full pound of pasta and the entire loaf of bread—and begged for his dinner an hour later. Ben just didn't do things like that, having a reputation as a serious and sober hunting dog to consider. And we weren't going to be gone long.

We had planned to grab and go, but ran into friends and sat for a bit. When we came up to the car, Adriana stopped transfixed. "Look at what they've done!" she cried.

We thought we'd put everything edible where the dogs couldn't get it. Everything but the expensive pancake mix we were planning on for a special Sunday breakfast. Buddy, our Cocker, stood over the torn apart box. The back of my van looked like an arctic snowfield. Buddy's jaws dripped long drools of pancake paste, Ben's Chocolate Lab face was coated with flour and paste and he was laboriously trying to work a big hunk of sticky dough out of his lower lip like a baseball player with a big chaw of Red Man. He looked like an explosion in the Oreo factory.

Buddy's now heavily starched ears were starting to harden like cement. Flour was an inch deep on the floor. There was pancake paste on the steering wheel, crusting the carpeting, stuck to the dashboard, gobbed on the front seat, and spattered on the speedometer, the

"Buddy told me it was a good idea."

headliner, the door panels and windshield.

We looked at the mess and wanted to cry—and kill both of those fools. Then we looked at each other and our two idiotic dog children and laughed until our sides hurt.

You learn to adjust to things. I could knit a sweater out of hair shed by our son Ryan's dog, Rusty. Rusty's our daycare dog and with us almost constantly. So is his hair. We comb it out by the grocery bagful. It falls out on its own by the bushel. We try to take good care of him. By mid-January it will be cold and Rusty could well be totally bald. I'm sure I'll notice the chilly temperature.

He should be glad to have the sweater. It will be cozy. We'll have a fire going in the family room fireplace and all sit around kitchen table and have pancakes. If Adriana bought some more of that fancy pancake mix.

Dick

Seattle, Washington

Hark!

The advent

Christmas is coming. It rang like a golden Pavlov's bell in the heart of every kid. It happened without reminders from television. That hadn't been invented yet. Nor were we tipped off by Christmas tree lights appearing in September on drug store shelves. Those still carried mostly fearful stuff like cod liver oil and rubber hot water bottles with strange attachments.

But somehow, a bit before Halloween, we *knew*, with an instinct as sure as geese mysteriously compelled to fly south. It was coming soon and our lives would all take on a different flavor. The egg salad sandwich existence of grade school would be transformed. At least for a little while wild hopes stood a chance of being fulfilled.

Maybe it was the unexplained stuff showing up in

the kitchen. I still don't have any idea what citron is or where it comes from. But suddenly the kitchen smelled a little bit like fruitcake—and I heard the first faint tinkle of the bell.

The Ladies all baked in those pre-WWII days. And those who turned to cake mixes would have been ousted from the Haller Lake Grade School PTA had they been found out. "Have you heard about Mrs. Larsen? Her poor children…"

Increased baking activity, along with shopping bags that got hustled into the bedroom behind a door that was otherwise never locked, announced the Christmas season. Not the holiday season mind you, because Thanksgiving was mostly about eating and drawing pictures of Pilgrims and trying to get out of being one in the school pageant. Christmas was about magic.

And a part of Seattle that isn't there anymore was about to be transformed. And we were about to be touched by the phenomenon that made every kid rich, magnified by the fact that virtually none of us were.

My parents were immigrants from the far eastern German province of Pomerania. Many of our neighbors, most of whom were so scattered that we could not see their houses, were immigrants from Norway, Sweden, Finland, Ireland, and Italy. And if they were born here, their parents' language was sometimes still spoken at the table—and used to discuss Christmas shopping in front of kids who hadn't learned it.

The road in front of our house, just two miles north of Northgate Mall, was dirt. And Northgate wasn't there anyway. It was being farmed by industrious Japanese families.

In that time, people "dropped in." They came with tiny wild blackberries they'd picked. Or peaches they'd canned. Or giant dahlias they'd raised. Or some miniature chicken eggs from their "bantie" hens. And they'd stay for dinner.

But at Christmas time the complexion of these friendly trade goods changed. Ordinary groceries became extraordinary goodies. Mrs. Sloan nee' Scavatto turned out a fantastic Italian confection as light as air itself and *biscotti*. Mrs. Nielsen manufactured *stollen*. My mother spent late nights making endless *pfeffernüsse*, a cookie that looked like a musket ball. They were baked weeks ahead of time and put away for later. Aged to be almost tooth-breaking hard, they were a favorite of coffee lovers and dunkers all over Haller Lake.

Pfeffernüsse. Achingly sweet and hard as bullets to test the strongest jaw.

During these marathon baking sessions the air would become powdered sugar sweet—to me the first scent of Christmas. In fact, if I were going to write the recipe for the smells of Christmas back then the ingredients would be something like—

Powdered sugar
Vanilla
Douglas Fir
Cinnamon
Library paste and construction paper
The starch in my sister's pinafore
Shoe polish
Foggy mornings
Brilliantine and Mr. Evan's barbershop
Soft, sputtering candle flame…

and the toy department in the Bon Marche right next to where the only *real* Santa Claus reigned, despite what the Frederick and Nelson advocates said.

Of course He, and I capitalize *He* because of His all-seeing nature, brought out a whole season of soul-searching for each of us. We began to seriously re-examine the whole notion of "being good" and wonder if we had accumulated enough points. It was perhaps even harder then than now because we had to reckon on obsolete factors like "obedience," now politically incorrect and no longer uttered, and "duty," which meant that feeding Mooly our cow and splitting kindling for ancient Mrs. Nelson every Thursday took precedence over personal agendas no matter how much you didn't like it.

These ponderings were reinforced by stories many mothers read to potentially delinquent youths. Quite different than children's books now, they often dealt with rude, ill-mannered and unthinking boys who met a bad end. I took them very seriously. I was also certain that Santa Claus did.

I also worried that we didn't have a proper chimney. Ours ended in a pot-bellied wood heater in our living room. Too warm a welcome for the jolly old elf. But we had a back-up tradition, because in Germany nobody came down the chimney except chimney sweeps.

Our Christmas was really Christmas Eve, "Holy Evening" in German. After church we'd come home to cookies, rich homemade eggnog, and our tree trimmed with fragile ornaments from the old country, paper angels from Sunday School, tons of tinsel, and garlands my sister had made in the third grade. On top of it all, a fragile and pointed glass "topper" as magnificent to me as the tower of any famous cathedral I've since seen anywhere.

In a tattered box somewhere I still have one or two clip-on holders left from my earliest childhood when our tree was trimmed with real candles. You couldn't leave the room when they were lit, and you would never have Smokey Bear as a guest, but their gleam is still dancing around in my memory.

And then we'd sing. My mother would begin in her tentative, wavering singing voice, with carols from her childhood. We chimed in with our own favorites from Away in a Manger to O Come All Ye Faithful, and O Tannenbaum in German, although I didn't know what all the words meant. Then my father would finally begin, *"Stille Nacht, Heilige*

Nacht…" in his measured baritone. Silent Night. Holy Night. Christmas was here.

Then we'd be shooed into the kitchen to wait. Endlessly. We could hear murmuring. We could hear paper rattling. We could hear giggling and my mother saying, "August, stop that." And then we'd hear the sound of a bell. Pavlov's bell. Then it was just like Christmas is for every kid today. Once again Santa escaped without us seeing him.

But we were left with much more than the gifts under the tree. I hope you are, too. It's a wonderful time of the year. Put some of it away in your heart for later.

Dick

Seattle, Washington

"Love, Joey"

When I was little, our dog, Schnappsy, got lost. My older brother searched the streets and woods for him for days, calling and calling. He finally found him dead at the bottom of an abandoned well.

The valiant little black and white dog, the offspring of a fox terrier and a dachshund, had fallen through rotten boards that covered the yawning mouth of a forgotten well long concealed by dank ferns, tough old salal plants and blackberry vines that were common in our sparsely settled rural neighborhood. He must have paddled mightily, scratching at the sides of the well until cold, fear and fatigue finally seized his heart.

Years later I knew exactly how he must have felt alone in the dark, fighting against hopelessness, yet hoping against hope that the darkness would yield to a flashlight and that a hand would reach out to him. I fell into a well of another kind. In 1981 my wife of 26 years succumbed to the ravages of an incurable cancer.

Just yesterday I received a note from a longtime friend and the anguish that poured out in his letter about his recent divorce summed up and mirrored my life at that desperate low point now long ago. "I've never lived alone," he wrote. "Went right from home to the seminary, to the Army, then to marriage." Me, too.

Have you ever watched a lost dog in your neighborhood? They run up and down the street, darting from house to house and frantically up and down driveways, trying to find something or someone familiar. If they are lucky, they don't get hit by cars or fall down wells. But they are suddenly alone and it feels awful.

In my grief I was in a well. I could hear what I thought might be distant words. They were probably kind, well-intentioned words of sympathy and compassion. But I couldn't make them out as their distorted syllables echoed at the bottom of my well. No kind of logic about grief "passing away with time" or being in a "better place" registered with me any more than the wind whistling through the leaves or the patter of rain falling on the broken boards that covered my well—even though today I would say that I believe and understand those things and appreciate them. The water that was trying to envelop me was too cold and I was too frightened.

Obviously I am no longer in that place. I can vividly remember when suddenly something pierced my darkness. It came from a little kid, the son of my friend, Jim Gerlitz. It was a picture Joey drew, the one you see here. Jim, a wonderful father, must have spoken about me at home to his family. He handed me Joey's picture and said, "Joey wants me to give you this and tell you he loves you."

I have no way to explain how that simple gesture from a child suddenly illuminated my darkness and lifted my heart to solid ground. I've kept and treasured that message, "Love, Joey" for years. I can't remember whether the drawing is supposed to be me or Joey. It doesn't matter because for a moment in my heart we were part of one another.

Of course I'm no longer alone in the dark. I have a wonderful marriage that has blessed me for years and a great family who have changed everything for me. I know they'll never let go of me because they wrap me in love. They're a part of me. And I'll never let go of them either, because I know how it feels. Cold and frightening.

Today Joe Gerlitz is one of the best advertising writers in the city. I am now merely one of the *oldest*. I know Joe has won a lot of awards, but the best thing he ever wrote was "Love, Joey."

If I could, I'd also give him a trophy for art direction and illustration—and lifesaving.

Dick

Seattle, Washington

"And now these three remain: faith, hope and love. But the greatest of these is love."
—*1 Corinthians 13:13*

> the Queen now wore the most provocative dresses, even
> ls. She hung some extremely indelicate pictures on the
> ad fig leaves removed from its statues; and when the Pope
> istrate with her both about this and her refusal to make
> nversion, she merely replied that she was not in the least
> ons worthy only of priests'. It was rumoured that she was
> ɔm she had met in a convent in the Campo Marzio; and it
> reason, that she had fallen in love with Cardinal Azzolino.
> ̇hristina was to leave Rome for a time was accordingly
> ᵉ papal Court.
>
> of power and hoping to solve her financial problems, she
> self made Queen of Naples. But her schemes foundered;

Read any good books lately?

Last Sunday morning I was standing in our kitchen reading the back of a Honey Nut Cheerios box while waiting for the coffee maker to make its final burp and tell me my first cup of coffee was ready. The Sunday newspaper was already on the table waiting for me to sit down, but I'd become engrossed in the cereal box story of Buzz, the bee who won a crucial baseball came with a sticky fastball.

Just in case you are wondering, I am a college graduate with a degree in German literature, a grandfather, a respected member of our community, and just a few weeks ago lectured a marketing and advertising class at a leading local university.

But beyond, and perhaps in spite of, all those things, I am a reader. I read everything in front of me. I read ingredients statements on packaged pasta. I read cab drivers' hack licenses posted in the back seat of taxis. I read the lists of horrendous side effects that come with prescription pills. Buzz, the bee, was just one of an infinitely long list of things I have been reading for as long as I can remember.

I'm not sure when my obsession with reading started. I'm relatively sure it was kicked off when my mother read stories and the comics to me. She read Sunday school lessons and I still remember patricidal Absalom whose long hair tangled in the branches of an oak tree where he was killed. I remember Struwwelpeter (Messy Peter), a horrible boy whose hair was never cut and whose fingernails were never trimmed. I got the idea, even though the story was in German I could not understand. My mother's stories always had a sharp and uncomfortable point. Painful or not, I could hardly stand to wait to learn how these tales came out and knew *I must read.*

I recall sounding out letters in Miss Hansen's first grade class, the travails of Dick and Jane, and then finally My Weekly Reader, the little kid's version of the New York Times. I was off and running.

My brother, ten years older than I, introduced me to the downtown Seattle Public Library, a half hour bus ride from home. It was overflowing with books and I was overwhelmed. "How am I going to read all of these?" It was a challenge worthy of Greek mythology. I gave it a shot.

Fred left me in the Humor section, which became

my home base. I scarfed up H. Allen Smith, Robert Benchley, James Thurber, S.J. Perelman and Mark Twain. I shrieked out loud with laughter until a Librarian, a fearsome figure, told me to shut up.

Along the way a family friend gave me a book called Rud Riley and the Four Aces, a flying story from World War I. I branched out into thrillers. I dived into Stevenson's Black Arrow, which my father had bought for me when I was about five and well before I could really read. I kept coming back to it until I finally could. It was a *real book*, thick and full of words I had to look up. It was *work,* but I was glowing inside when I finally read it.

Everything was fair game. Even Dr. Morris Fishbein's Home Medical Adviser in our bookcase next to the World Atlas, a popular reference book of the time, which convinced me I had symptoms of most of the diseases it discussed from appendicitis to psoriasis (with pictures of a horrid rash.) And it opened my young eyes with actual diagrams of vaginas that I contemplated with newly discovered scientific interest.

On Saturdays my sister Diane and I would take trips downtown, often to the library from which we would bring home as many books as each of us could carry, particularly during the summer, in our view a season created for playing and reading.

If our mother happened to be with us she was always good for a bacon, lettuce and tomato sandwich at the Rexall Drug Store or a trip to

Woolworth's where I would persuade her to buy me one or more Big Little Books, fat little adventure books that had pictures in the upper right corner that would make "movies" when you flipped the pages. My all-time favorite was "Maximo Miller. The Amazing Super Man." He generated high voltage electricity long before anybody thought of the sticky fingered spider web guy.

At home we had magazines like The Country Gentleman, slanted toward rural readers but with some great writers such as Burton Hillis and Ellis Parker Butler and covers by Norman Rockwell, N.C. Wyeth and other outstanding artists. All this literary and painterly artistry vied with ads for Bag Balm for chapped cow teats and little blinders to put on chickens that pecked one another to death.

Suddenly it all came to a halt. High school had arrived. Reading was no longer fun, it was mandatory. Somewhere, high up in The Scheme of Things, some authority decided that I must read things like My Antonia, a book that still makes me gag.

When Little House on the Prairie came along later on television, which hadn't been invented yet, I couldn't watch it. It seemed to be My Antonia revisited. It's possible that the books dictated by the powers that be caused some kind of glandular dyspepsia in my now much more important boy parts. But I simply did not want to read much of anything for almost three years. I was saved by a miracle, one much scoffed at by the literary elite.

My blessed mother got a subscription to the Reader's digest. I didn't particularly want to read it, but then I discovered that after each short story there were *jokes*. I couldn't resist them; then I idly read a story or two. The tale of a daring escape from a POW camp. The invention of the ball point pen. A rags to riches business tale. How much more real and interesting they seemed than My Antonia and The Junior Scholastic magazines at school.

They restarted my motor and it has not stopped since.

Words on paper hold a spellbinding attraction for me. It's not always good because I can easily lose myself reading even if I am with my wife whom I love more than life itself. My eyes are like a compass needle drawn by a magnet when in my peripheral vision I catch sight of a headline or a page of type beckoning like cocaine to an addict.

I now make thrice yearly trips to the Seattle Library book sales that burst the seams of an old aircraft hanger at the former Sand Point Naval Air Station near us with thousands of books for sale for as little as 25 cents. Each time I come home with 50 or 75 or 100 volumes to feed my habit of reading some three a week.

On my new iPhone I just downloaded 50 books for ten dollars, so I can read in the doctor's office where the magazines are often years old or while sitting in the car waiting for Adriana who has run into some store "for just a minute." I'm currently working on The Call of the Wild, which I have now read only a bit of in three-minute installments so far. The software also includes some books like Little Women, which I do not plan to read. It absolutely does not include My Antonia. I would have to sell my ultra cool phone.

Television hasn't helped encourage reading; the reverse is true, and I feel very sad about that. I like to go around saying "Anything worth doing is worth overdoing." That's just sort of smarty pants talk of course, and isn't really right. I can overdo reading and that's not good. But reading actually is magic and words have the power to fill corners of your life with ideas, understanding, and illumination like nothing else.

In the Bible, the apostle John declares "in the beginning was the Word and the Word was with God and the Word was God."

Who am I to argue with that?

Dick

Seattle, Washington

$$y = \frac{g\sec^2\theta}{2V_0^2} x^2 + x\tan\theta$$

Wing tips

The wing tip of the Alaska Airlines 737-800 on the tarmac in front of us curved upward in a graceful swoop. I'd seen the same wing shape before when watching a mallard instantaneously warp the tips of its wing feathers while negotiating a tight turn on its final approach before extending its air brakes and dropping feet first into a pond filled with cattails.

Earlier 737s didn't sport the turned up wing tip. It was the product of advancing aeronautical technology and countless hours of research before it emerged from a huge factory filled with engineers, and specialized workers of all kinds.

The duck on the other hand came out of an egg, much like the one on your breakfast table. It emerged as a little ball of yellow fluff with flat, webbed feet, and not looking much like it was destined for life in the air. Yet in just weeks, even before its downy fuzz had sprouted all its final feathers, it would be aloft.

It took our son Peter some $60,000 and two years of hard work to qualify as a pilot and secure a commercial pilot's license. The young duck got no perceivable instruction, no flights with an instructor, no ground school classes, no lessons in taking off, landing, handling spins or understanding weather conditions. Yet there it was, a little clumsy at first, but in just days mastering twisting, dodging aerial turns that would defy the pilot of an F-18 fighter for their flawless, lightning fast execution.

Watch a startled mallard suddenly explode vertically from the water, faster than most hunters can follow it with a shotgun and you realize that Britain's vaunted Harrier vertical take-off fighter bomber is turtle-like in comparison.

Today our most sophisticated combat jets rely on computers to even remain stable in the air. In the attempt to enhance their ability to do maneuvers a duck never has to think about, aeronautical engineers have created machines so complex that even the most skilled pilots can't fly without computerized assistance. Even then, human brains and muscles can barely respond fast enough to perform the evasive and strategic moves demanded by aerial combat as pilots are pushed to the edge of their abilities.

A greenwing teal however, a duck only a bit bigger than a pigeon, can seemingly dodge birdshot traveling at over the speed of sound, and streak off untouched with just a flick of its eye and a shrug of its wings. I've seen it happen. No computer, no Top Gun School. Just the miracle of genetics formed in the yolk of an egg. Wow.

Instead of that silly sailor suit perhaps Donald Duck should wear the gold stripes of a senior pilot—not just four, but about 20 on each sleeve. Despite the wonders that come from the remarkable efforts of humans, and all the acclaim and awards we congratulate ourselves with, our works are infinitely tinier and less significant than those of our Creator.

Oh, and the upturned wingtip? I think it's called a "canard." If I'm not mistaken, that's the French word for—*duck*.

Dick

Aboard Alaska Airlines
Flight 728 to Tucson.

Whatever happened to holidays?

To most of the people I know from middle age on down, the word *holiday* now just means "day off."

It's not just those big red-letter days on the calendar. It's even days like Cinco de Mayo and St. Patrick's Day. One marks a battle bravely fought against a powerful foreign army, the other a slave who became a saint. Today both are mostly about drinking beer, one with nachos and the other with corned beef and cabbage. Lincoln and Washington's birthdays have been smooshed together in an ecumenical Presidents' Day.

I think the new generation is missing something. Things like a tingle down the spine, a catch in the throat, a rush of overwhelming gratitude, the inexplicable thrill of sudden goose bumps, and emotions that suffused your entire being with love, pride, or awe.

There was a time when days like Armistice Day hadn't yet become our all-purpose Veterans Day, but still evoked the choking, lung-searing fire of poison gas, the acrid stink of cordite, and the cries of wounded men in the foreign forests of the Argonne in WWI.

When, and if, you came home from that, Thanksgiving Day meant something far more than a day of football. Less than 25 years down the road from WWI we were again at war and in my school classroom we sang the Marines' Hymn and Anchors Aweigh. As we made cardboard Pilgrim hats and cut out paper autumn leaves we were taught that Thanksgiving was about thankfulness to God for keeping our forebears alive through the winter. Both of my parents, like those of many of my classmates, came to America from another country. Yet when your dad was out of work, as my boilermaker father often was in the pre-war depression, it wasn't hard to identify with those earlier immigrants.

Like those Pilgrims, our neighbors too clung together and we found plenty of food for our table. One year it might be a tough and ancient hen that my softhearted father had allowed to live far beyond her laying years. He finally handed my mother the axe and looked the other way. Once he traded a neighbor for two sizeable turkeys who were immediately murdered by our giant Rhode Island Red rooster who found them strutting among *his* harem.

We had our Thanksgiving dinner early that year. But our prayers were

Turkeys are noted for their good taste, but relatively poor judgement.

still laced with gratitude and astonishment at our fortune as bowls of steaming hot stuffing, mashed potatoes, sweet potatoes, green garden beans, fresh corn and homemade biscuits followed one another onto our table. I'd split the cedar kindling, my brother had cut the cord wood for our wood stove, and my sister had set the table, but it was my mother who got all the glory right after we'd given God his due.

Mama had never seen a turkey, a sweet potato or a pumpkin pie in Germany, and corn was fed only to livestock. But when she came here she worked hard to become an American. She never lost her accent, but I think you would have felt right at home at our table. Except maybe when we passed the red cabbage. That had a German accent, too.

I can't recall us eating in restaurants as we grew up. Dinner with friends and church potlucks were the feasts I remember. In those years we began to see empty places at family tables and in the pews of our little church. Red bordered flags with blue stars hung on many front doors, whispering somberly that someone was away in the service. Sometimes the blue stars were replaced with gold ones and we knew that Billy, or Ted or Evelyn, the Army nurse, were not coming back.

The mothers consoled one another, but they also had much work to do, even though few had jobs in that era. My mother and many neighbor ladies took on Civil Defense assignments. As my mother studied the preamble of the Constitution for her citizenship test, she also shuffled a deck of silhouettes of Japanese warplanes since she was a volunteer aircraft spotter. Her station was the tower of Lakeside School, at that time surrounded by woods and an occasional house in rural North Seattle. She walked there on Thursday nights, guided by a flashlight and rehearsing aloud, "We the people of the United States, in order to form a more perfect union…" Like many women in our neighborhood, she didn't drive. Most families had only one car anyway and that one went to work.

On other evenings we gathered in the living room—my father harrumphing over the newspaper, my sister doing her homework, I writing to my brother, now in the Army. And my mother was reading over and over again an inconceivable message from her mother in Germany, saying that all our family there were well and sent love to us. Somehow the Red Cross and those 10 or 15 words pasted in strips telegram-style on a tiny piece of paper had connected another family across the great gulf of a divided world. In the background, on the radio, Bing Crosby was singing a song we ached to believe in, promising "I'll be home for Christmas" and looking forward to reunion with snow and mistletoe and presents on the tree. We cherished that promise, even if, like in that hope-filled world of song, it were only in our dreams.

Even on July 4, 1945 when we stood to salute the passing flag and marching troops in downtown Seattle, we had no idea the Emperor of Japan would broadcast a surrender message ending the war just 43 days later. But we had faith and pride in our country and its destiny as its anthem resonated in our hearts.

Then December was here and for most of us those Christmas dreams had come true. Along the way my future brother-in-law appeared in church, resplendent in a uniform glittering with ribbons and decorations from combat on Okinawa. My sister prayed he would look her way and a couple of years later he did—for the rest of his life in a long, loving marriage.

My brother too came home alive and well and our blue star still hangs in my office today to remind me to remember things that I will never forget anyway.

No camera could capture the

magic of that long-awaited peacetime Christmas. Though if you could look into my memories, you could see the tree, hear the songs, feel the hugs and smell the scents from the kitchen.

It was no ordinary day off. It was a real holiday in another time and another world.

Dick

Seattle, Washington

"Learn from the mistakes of others. You can't live long enough to make them all yourself."

Cogito ergo zoom

It was like one of those spy stories. where the skulking Communist deep cover agent has waited for 25 years in Washington, D.C. to be activated by a coded message from his spy masters in the Kremlin. He's read the Washington Post classifieds daily for decades so he doesn't miss it: *"For sale. Antique harpoon mfd. 1843 in New Bedford. Write Box 231."*

In my case, I'd only had to wait about four years, combing the Seattle Times classifieds every morning. "What are you looking for?" the Professoressa would ask me. "Uh…um, nothing…do you think it will rain today?" I'd say, being artfully fast on my feet.

I was in denial. Alcoholics always say they're just social drinkers. Fat people claim they just have big bones. I couldn't just blurt out that I had contracted a serious malady in Italy, more serious than picking up a tropical parasite or a run-of-the-mill social disease.

An Italian doctor would have diagnosed it as a persistent and embarrassing dose of *scooterosis nervosa*. It's characterized by staring bug-eyed at passing two-wheelers ridden by signorinas with beautiful legs and raven black hair blowing in the wind—and not noticing the signorina, at least not first. Or seeing oneself in James Bond's tuxedo, holding a long barreled automatic pistol with a silencer and posing coolly with a beautiful blue scooter. Or in Italian, *il scooter*.

The mental picture had obsessed me for years, but I never spoke of it. *I wanted a Vespa.* No, I desperately craved one. In my heart I knew knew without doubt that my message would come. It came on a Saturday. When I knocked and Cory Smith came to the door he looked like anything but a courier. I gave him the identifying phrase I'd waited years to say: "Hi, I'm Dick, (swallow) I saw your ad—you've got the Vespa, I've got the money." That was the easy part. It was harder when I got home. Adriana had thought I'd just gone to the store to get a gallon of skim milk. I actually ended up going later. My new little cobalt blue Vespa was perfect for zipping up to the Safeway. It turned heads, especially mine.

This story could well have ended at this point and right now you could be looking at my James Bondish picture in tuxedo and scooter. But instead that dream scenario somehow lurched into gear all by itself and went roaring off in an unexpected direction, taking me with it. I came down with a serious complication, MPS (More Power Syndrome.) The same thing that drives kayakers to twin screw yachts and Prius drivers to Chrysler Hemis.

Like Audrey Hepburn in Roman Holiday, Adriana fancied riding with me on the back of my Vespa. We made several sorties that way, but little 50 cc scooters are not made to zoom up hills carrying two people, unless both are seriously anorexic. Just a few months later I almost magically found myself the owner of a man-size Vespa Gran Turismo 200. Enough speed and torque to leave teenagers in their daddys' Mustangs behind at the stoplight. Enough power to ride double with the Incredible Hulk's bigger brother and not slow down.

We both loved it. We went touring with friends in the evening and parked on the sidewalk at Tutta Bella for pizza. We cruised through the Arboretum at sunset and stopped for a glass of wine outside Sostanza in Madison Park as the gulls wheeled over Lake Washington. Adriana got to play Audrey Hepburn, except the law no longer allowed passengers to ride side saddle like the movie princess.

In Italy I even bought an exact scale model of this lovely machine and carried it around with me traveling, so I could insert it into photographs wherever we went like Alfred Hitchcock's famous cameo appearances in his own movies.

Vespa means "wasp" in Italian, a feminine noun, so according to Italian usage all Vespas should have feminine names. I dubbed mine *Bella Mia*. However, it was hard to remember, because at stoplights I couldn't help hollering, "Hi Yo, Silver. Awaayyyy!" in sheer joy.

Then disaster struck. While riding on a tree-lined highway winding around scenic Hood Canal we hit a patch of gravel on a blind curve and flew into a ditch. I was knocked unconscious, my beloved Vespa was destroyed and worse yet, Adriana had a badly broken ankle that took a titanium plate, nine screws and many months of painful healing to repair.

The course of conventional wisdom probably would have been to say goodbye to scooters. I had already given up on my fancied James Bond/Gregory Peck image. But it was replaced by a gnawing fear, one that I couldn't see learning to live with. I bought a new scooter, an Aprila Scarabeo GT 500. Bigger and faster, a lot faster. When I first got on it, I felt like I was climbing aboard a killer Brahma bull in a rodeo chute. Gradually the fear subsided, replaced by deep respect. Adriana won't get on it with me; she still has bad dreams about our accident.

Now I can go 96 mph on the freeway, but I won't. They say that if you fall off a horse, you should get back on. That's what I did. I am extremely careful about riding my new steed and no longer holler "HiYo Silver!"

I miss Adriana on the back of the seat, but I won't

coax her to join me. I know how she feels. That was a stiff price to pay for the sense of freedom a scooter or motorcycle offers. I still have the pleasure of the wind in my face and the rush of the road ahead, a joy she no longer has. I wish it were not so, but if wishes were motor scooters, beggars would ride.

Philosopher and mathematician René Descartes famously proclaimed "Cogito ergo sum." *I think, therefore I am.* He obviously hadn't yet acquired a good scooter. If he had waited awhile to get a little bit more out of life, or maybe taken a few more chances, he might have gotten that Latin phrase closer to being right.

To zoom or not to zoom, that is the question...

Dick

Seattle, Washington

The Duck Blind
A hunting club at South Bend

Open season

Hunters are a distinctive lot, but quite unlike those other more refined folks who claim to be fly fishermen. It is not my purpose here to denigrate fly fishermen. They contribute huge amounts to our economy, investing in replicas of insects, graphite fly rods more costly than a pretty good used car, and funny looking tweedy clothing that they order at great expense from the Orvis catalog so they can look like aristocratic British gamekeepers, Lord Chumleigh-Ralston and all that.

Hunters are, well, to put it bluntly, more *gamey* and, goodness knows, often dirtier. That comes from falling into muddy-banked irrigation ditches in a farmer's field or stepping into cow pies that he carelessly allows his bovine employees to leave all over the place.

Fly fishing is nice and clean. Artistic people like authors and rich movie stars do it. It is relatively non-violent too. Fly fishing people simply seek to annoy the fish, sinking sharp, barbless hooks into their lips, wrenching them out of their watery homes and then twisting the hooks out of their mouths with little Orvis pliers they carry on retractable reels pinned to their Orvis vests next to their retractable Orvis nail nippers and their retractable Orvis magnifying glass that helps them tie their dainty replica insects (Orvis) to the tippets of their Orvis fly lines.

A somewhat lower class of fly fisherpersons are outfitted by L.L. Bean, which is as functionally fashionable as Orvis, but just a tad less Anglified, old chap. It is said that many Hollywood celebrities and hangers-on consider an outdoor adventure to be ordering something from the L.L. Bean catalog.

In contrast, hunters are mostly clad by Walmart and K-Mart or Big 5 until they become successful enough to buy their floppy waders, camouflage hats with ear flaps, and soon to be grungy and ripped jackets from some fellows named Cabela, whose stores are veritable zoos of stuffed dead animals like Bambi, Flipper and Tony the Tiger. Fly fishermen put their quarry back in the water after they are done tormenting it. They call it sporting. Hunters kill their game and eat it. They call it delicious.

I have some empathy for fly fishermen and for a time advocated a shoot and release program and hunting ducks with barbless shot. After shooting them I would throw them back into the air and cry, "You're free! Fly off. Fly off!" The ducks would not cooperate and there was then little I could do other than marinate their breasts, which I smoked over alder chips, sliced thin and served as hors d'oeuvres with toasted sesame seeds and hot Chinese mustard .

Fly fishers may have a passion for their sport, but it is a cool, reserved and intellectual passion that adds a ballet-like element aura to their sport. How different that is from the life and death of young hunter I knew named Dave. I frequently hunted some years ago with my friend Harry and his son, Gus. Gus came hunting with us from maybe age ten until he was in his twenties. In those later years Gus had his own hunting partner, a kid his own age named Dave. It was clear early on that both Gus and Dave were born to hunt. Then one day Dave found out he had an inoperable and deadly brain tumor.

We lost Dave. But no effete ballet drama for Dave. Before he died Dave made arrangements with an ammunition company to load his ashes into shotgun shells, which were his last bequest to his friends. "Take these with you," he wrote them, "Wherever you hunt, shoot them up so I can keep hunting with you." Dave traveled all over the world hunting with those friends who carried out his last wish.

We hunters, bird and duck hunters at any rate, are more distinguished by our dogs than we are by the cut of our jackets, the brand of our shotguns, or the origin of the tons of gear we accumulate. Oddly, to a large degree, it is our dogs that confer upon us our pedigrees, not looking like English lords, African safari guides, or Bengal Lancers in off-duty knickers. In this respect I was initially sadly disadvantaged. While I'd grown up with a hunting dog, I was, after my marriage, sadly dogless for some years. Then, to crack my late wife's resistance to owning a mutt, I bought her a miniature poodle. How my hunting buddies laughed when I stuffed him in the back pocket of my game coat and took him pheasant hunting in eastern Washington. I'd like to say that it was like that old ad with the headline, *"They laughed when I sat down at the piano, but when I began to play..."* But it didn't work out like that. Tino had a good time, I didn't.

The laughter continued when Tino was gone and I got a full-sized Standard Poodle. But I had a secret. My buddies didn't know that poodles were originally bred for duck hunting in Germany. They got Frenchified later. I trained Candy and she became my retriever. The remarks about rhinestone collars and painted toe nails died away when she found and retrieved pheasants and swam to fetch downed ducks in ponds and water-filled ditches.

Unfortunately, this princess of a dog was delicately lady-like in her approach to things. Instead of launching herself like an artillery round into the water like a Lab, she'd walk to its edge, and feel the bottom with a tentative paw, declining to swim after game if the bottom felt uncomfortably mushy.

I once shot a large Canada goose that crashed to the

ground just ahead of us. I sent Candy to fetch it, a 10 pound mouthful for a slim 60 pound dog. She grabbed it, but the bird wasn't dead. It started screaming, beating her about the head with its huge wings. She spit it out, ran back and sat down *behind* me. "Are you out of your mind," she seemed to say angrily. "We're not doing this."

My first Chocolate Lab, Dutch, put me back on an even footing reputation-wise with my buddies. When duck hunting near the little town of South Bend in coastal western Washington we always stayed with our dogs, (Poodle, Labs, Golden Retrievers, Brittany Spaniels) in the shabby H&H motel. Filled with duck hunters during the season, the beds at the H&H were always covered with guys, dogs, decoys, wet socks, ammo, six packs of beer, and usually cigar ashes.

When Adriana and I married, I introduced her boys, Ryan and Peter, to the brotherhood of hunters and the H&H, after they'd taken appropriate Hunter Safety Training classes conducted by the state game department. I'm not sure which they liked best, our time in the field or the mammoth breakfasts in the H&H coffee shop, heavy on the grease, please.

The first time Adriana stayed with us for a weekend in the H&H was the beginning of the end. She hated the way it smelled. She hated that the rooms had no phones or TVs. She hated the mildew in the bathroom and the rusty water that ran out of the shower. She hated our prized gourmet guy food in the coffee shop. It took no persuasion at all to get her to agree to look around for "a place where I could build a little duck shack."

What I had in mind was a simple little number out of plywood, with an outhouse in the back. After all, we were only going to sleep there. Silly me. It became five acres on the Willapa Bay waterfront and a two bedroom, one bath cottage complete with dishwasher, fridge, washer and dryer, gas fireplace in the great room, and a porch as wide as the house with rustic furniture and a swing that would seat three so we could swing while we looked over the bay with a glass of wine in one hand. Dogs were allowed in the house, but they had to sleep on the floor. The upside was that the food suddenly became much better than at the late lamented H&H.

To the dogs it was also heaven. Dutch or Ben could swim as much as they wanted without being expected to retrieve anything. Buddy, our Cocker could honor his hidden Wild Dog nature by galloping along the beach and wallowing in sticky mud puddles until you couldn't tell whether he was a dog, a racoon, a bear cub or a giant mudball with a vibrating tail.

At night we were alone with a heaven full of stars and the sound of distant coyotes calling or the near silent swish of the wings of bats or nighthawks competing for insects in the dark. In the daytime we marveled at elk or deer standing in our yard, bald eagles silhouetted in the tops of the trees, or rabbits bursting out of the underbrush.

The cabin and the dogs, except for our old friend Buddy, are gone now. On the walls of one room in our house hang several sets of collars, tags and dog whistles, the artifacts of treasured times gone by. I no longer hunt and in a drawer are a sheaf of licenses saved from decades spent pursuing wild game in the fields.

Every time my just two-year-old granddaughter visits she immediately goes into the garage and brings two old decoys into the family room. I don't know what her fascination with them is. I hope it is something in her blood. She is already making Rusty, Ryan's dog who is with us most of the time, obey her so she can pet him. These are all good signs and I am thinking of getting her a small, cut-down shot gun when she is older, maybe three—if I can wait that long.

I'd at least like her to have it before somebody offers to take her fly fishing.

Dick

Seattle, Washington

The tenants

We figured they were just a couple of "Lookie-Loos", the real estate brokers' term for those who do endless window shopping for a place to live, while never getting around to making a decision. Some are just plain nosy folks who just like to see how others live.

Lookie-Loos critique the drapes, decry your interior decorating, and make insulting remarks about your taste, your housekeeping or the looks of your relatives they see in photos on your fireplace. But they never put their money where their malformed social behavior is.

She wasn't like that. Showing up first without her husband, she was modestly clad in gray, quiet and unassuming. We counted her to be an earthy type as the first thing she wanted to see was the garden, cocking her head and looking quizzically at bordering trees from top to bottom, at our three-tiered Italian fountain, and a little warily at our Cocker when Buddy first barked at her and then snubbed her by turning his back and peeing on a shrub. Her better half arrived moments after she did. "Now it starts—a wise guy," I thought, with a straw in his mouth, a slicked back black coiffure and a red vest that I sure wouldn't wear, even though I am no paragon of taste.

It dawned on me that she had a straw in her mouth, too. No, not a straw, a twig. Of course that is something robins do when they are building a nest. Then I realized that I'd seen them both before, individually, as they'd flown in and out of the yard in the past couple of days, sometimes stopping to splash in our fountain or checking out the potential of various trees around the yard. But this time was no idle inspection, this was moving day and it was for keeps. The trees had already been rejected as not offering enough cover, shelter or protection.

Their chosen destination was deep inside the tangled vines and leafy foliage of our grape arbor. They weren't first to pick this residential development. It had a history.

Some years back we decided to erect an arbor as sort of an archway over our patio table and chairs that we liked to use of a warm summer evening. We even hung attractive outdoor light fixtures in it to set the mood for a glass or two of wine and often a dinner for just the two of us, or with friends and family. Adriana of course wouldn't settle for just the bare wood arbor as spiffy as I thought it was. She wanted clematis, or wisteria or bougainvillea to climb its trellises. If we couldn't be in Italy, we could feel like we were. I'm not good at flowers. They have names that sound like "appendicitis" or "homophobia." I could hear some physician saying, "My god, woman, you have a terrible inflammation of your clematis."

Fortunately, we happened to visit a little outdoor craft and garden show with friends in Bellingham, where I discovered, in a little plastic pot, a hopeful looking young grapevine. "What is more Italian,?" I cried. Visions of designing my own proprietary wine label danced in my head. I could already see the huge, clusters of grapes hanging heavily awaiting harvest, crushing, barreling and bottling with our brand name in gold and friends panting for the gift of a bottle or two. Of course the vine was only a little stick about ten inches high.

We watered it, nurtured it and treated it to sips of Miracle-Gro. So it wouldn't be lonely Adriana also bought it a cousin, planted at the other end of the arbor. It was her vine vs. mine, and the Great Grape Race was on. They grew amazingly fast, climbing seven feet high and racing toward one another from opposite ends of the arbor. My vine won, I think, but you could hardly tell in the huge profusion of leaves that gave cool and lovely shade to our table below.

When I pruned the vines back the following spring I found a bird's nest that had been hidden in the leaves, where shade had protected it, breezes had caressed it, and the sun had kissed it. It was empty and we didn't know the story of those who had carefully put it there.

This time we vowed it would be different. These would be *our birds*. While we couldn't fly or sing their lovely songs, we would adopt them and be their grandparents—if we could do it without interfering with or altering their lives.

The Robins, we didn't know their first names, set to work building their nest in earnest, making trip after trip with such big loads of twigs, sticks, grass, and dried, spidery plant roots in their beaks that we wondered how they could fly. They tucked their nest away where they thought we couldn't see it. They hadn't reckoned on my step ladder and the long handled mirror I dragged out to see into their nest when they were out for lunch or whatever robins do when they aren't home. In due course there was one beautiful blue egg in the nest, then another and another.

Our outdoor life on the patio went on as theirs did above us in the grape foliage. One would sit on the eggs as we sat below them talking, eating and doing human carrying on, all while pretending hard that we weren't looking. But sometimes we would glance up and see the tip of a beak or a tight fan of tail feathers sticking out of the nest revealing Mr. or Mrs. on nest-tending duty.

Finally there was one little fledgling robin in the nest, a scrawny near naked creature that seemed to be all yellow beak and gray goose-pimpled skin dappled with sparse fuzz. Mom and Pop would appear once in awhile, one at a time, to bathe in our fountain, or to sit singing in a nearby tree, but most often we'd spot them in the air heading for the arbor with a beakful of a delicious daddy long legs, a wriggling worm or something else Junior and siblings we hadn't yet seen would eat. They'd even slip into their nest while we were eating right below them and trying hard not to look up.

Suddenly, for no apparent reason, there were no more flights, no heads looking over the edge of the nest, no little now-feathered robin perched on the rim of the nest thinking about leaping into a first flight. Finally I climbed my ladder and looked. One egg had completely disappeared. The shell fragments of another littered the bottom of the nest. Its inhabitant, the scrawny, fuzzy robin child lay cold and dead, his parents departed never to return. Maybe it was an attack by another bird or perhaps even a cat, but it was all over.

In time the leaves fell off leaving the empty nest starkly alone among the bare vines. After a time I carefully took it down and saved it for a long while until the weather started to warm up. Then I gently put it in a flowering tree by our front porch and put a tiny homemade For Rent sign on it. It was a fanciful piece of wishful thinking.

This fall our grapes bore practically no fruit at all and what was there was neither pretty nor edible. There was no new nest among the leaves and my rental offer went begging until the rain and the wind tore it from the tree by our front porch.

> **PORCHVIEW REALTY**
> Residences of Distinction
> **FOR RENT**
> One Bedroom
> Call Birdie Tweten
> **206-555-1212**

We're now empty nesters, too. Blessedly we've suffered no losses like our feathered friends. We also know that robins, new ones, will soon be back and with luck, a hummingbird or two. Real estate and life run in cycles. Some good and some bad.

Those old standbys—faith, hope and love—help even some small things average out in your favor.

Dick

Seattle, Washington

Grandpas Я us

That's my maternal grandfather, Gustav Rohde, feeding that sheep. The postcard photo was taken in the barn attached to the house where my mother was born in a tiny village in eastern Germany.

Photographs are as close as I ever got to any of my grandparents. My mother left home at 20 to marry my father and then live for the rest of her long life in America.

All through my childhood and even later my mother told me stories that made my grandparents come alive in my mind even though a depression and then World War II kept us separated. She told us of her father, a sober, religious man who was both a hardworking farmer and the village tailor. And she told us of my other grandfather who lived nearby,

Herman Paetzke, a handsome scalawag of a shoemaker who was a notorious consumer of alcoholic beverages. He was cashiered from the German army for striking an officer. His wife, my grandmother, was a midwife who attended the birth of my mother and hundreds of other babies born in the village and surrounded hamlets. My other grandmother was busy raising children; my mom was part of a family of nine siblings—Otto, Martin, Ewald, Gustav, Lisbeth, Anna, Ida, Frieda, and my mother, Gretchen. A full-time job.

Hermann Paetzke, two-fisted drinker

In time I came to know much about all of them all as my mother told us of her girlhood, life in the village, and of sisters and brothers I would never meet until years later when military service took me to Germany. By then my grandparents were long gone.

So I grew up grandparent-less and for many years that was okay with me. You don't really miss what you have never known. Aside from that my life seemed to be so different from what I saw in picture after sepia toned picture of a way of life that seemed so apart from what I was familiar with.

As the pictures and postcards and letters came over the years, I could see grandparents, cousins, aunts and uncles age, some die, some disappear for years into Soviet prisoner of war camps until years after the war had ended. In the constant tear and love-filled communications that went both ways I could see, but not really totally feel the depth of connection that existed between children and grandparents. I was, after all, also young and stupid and it took a long time to wear off. But one thing that never held the least little bit of appeal was the idea of being a grandfather.

That didn't come up for a very, very long time. My late first wife and I had no children. Unfortunately she couldn't have any and I simply didn't want any. If somebody said "father" to me, I knew they were talking about my dad. When Adriana and I married after my first long marriage, two boys came along as part of the package, so I tried to do the best fathering job I could as a stepdad, even though I never felt cut out for the work.

I think I was thunderstruck one day as the boys were approaching adulthood, when Adriana said something about becoming a grandparent. She had a funny, frighteningly radiant look on her face when she said it. She wanted it to happen. "Don't look at me," I protested, "I am not the grandpa type." She said, "Our grandchildren can call you 'Nonno', the Italian word for Grandpa."

"No. No." I cried, "Forget it. I don't even *like* children. I am not going to be anybody's Grandpa." And the picture of my grandfather, Gustav Rohde with the sheep, flashed across the screen of my consciousness. An old guy with a beard. Not me! Never me.

Even now after many years of crafting ads and television commercials, if I were to cast a TV spot with a prototypical grandparent in it, I would probably choose somebody who looked more like the late Paul Newman at 60, handsome, virile and gray-haired, than an actor resembling my own grandfathers who did indeed come from another place and another era. (I am, after all, considerably older than you are.) So at the very word a shiver ran through my core and I rushed off to pet the dog, as close as I wanted to get to any kind of offspring, particularly one that would turn me into one of them, a grandpa.

I was safe for almost 16 years. Adriana's women friends would occasionally blabber nonsense at me about looking forward to becoming a grandfather. It seemed to be a kind of feminine idiocy that was somehow built into their DNA. "Really," I'd scowl, "That's ridiculous. I am never going to be a grandfather, I don't like children. I don't even want to touch the icky little things. And don't even think about ever calling me Grandpa. End of subject."

I should have told our son Peter that.

On April 15 last year, Adriana's granddaughter was born. (Not *mine*, mind you. That kind of thing doesn't happen to me.) Giordana looked like Winston Churchill, except for the cigar, with lank, wet hair and a little red rash on her cheeks.

I did deign to take her picture. *And then somebody thrust her into my arms.* I had never before held a baby. I stood rigidly, frozen, a strange sensation, sort of a combination of fear that I would drop her and the same apprehension I had the first time I tried eating frog's legs. I gave her back in one minute 14 seconds, which would have been a pretty good time for staying on the back of a Brahma bull at the rodeo. I let out my breath—still alive. And she looked kind of cute.

I didn't see her again until about a week after she left the hospital with her parents. But something odd happened. That picture I took? I laminated it and put it my wallet. Normal, you say? Not for me. I have never carried pictures of my wife or kids, much to the consternation of my bride. It was just not me. Yet there I was whipping out this little kid's photo and showing it to people. Even making abrupt and disconnected detours in the conversation so I could bring the subject up. I confess, I even e-mailed it hither and yon, even though I knew nobody could possible care about this little red-faced child with her eyes clamped shut. I know, I know—but for some reason I couldn't help it.

That was the first step on a very slippery slope. After that it was all downhill. From then on I was lost, hopelessly hooked and totally, foolishly in love with this little being.

When I see her I rush to hold her on my lap. We play together with my office telephone and blabber Baby Martian, the language she speaks. I rock her to sleep and sing to her sometimes for an hour before her eyelids droop and she tucks her head against my chest and under my chin as her little arms go around my neck.

She is a music lover of widely diverse tastes, so I sing her Brahm's Lullaby in German, which my mother sang to me, the Marines' Hymn and the Army Field Artillery song, O Sole Mio in Italian, O My Darling Clementine, and Goodnight Irene. We play Italian CDs for children and she holds her skirt and dances to *"Buon giorno, buon giorno"* and a song about vowels—*A, E, I, O, U.*

I used to have a terrific crush on Cyd Cherise, she of the beautiful Long Legs, but her choreography has been replaced in my heart by Giordana's chunky-legged, fall-down-on-her-butt version. I am working on getting her to call me "Nonno"—or anything else I can understand. Heck, I'd even settle for *Grandpa.*

Since I started writing this some months ago, Adriana has been speaking to her almost entirely in Italian. She's rapidly learned many words.

When she must go home with her parents I bend down to her level as she stands by the door. "Bacio?" I ask her hopefully. When she plants that kiss on my lips and smiles, my heart skips a beat.

This may be the best time I have ever had. I suddenly feel connected to a whole new world, one that has been there all along that I couldn't touch.

I wonder what has happened. This is clearly not me, but I kind of like whoever it is.

Dick

Crawling around on the floor in
Seattle, Washington

"*Grandchildren are life's dessert.*"

Life without eyebrows

When I grew up, we didn't have indoor plumbing for some time. Like a number of our neighbors in what was then generally termed "the sticks," we had an outhouse, a simple structure situated beyond our garden, past the loganberry patch, and toward the back of our property way out by the chicken house.

On a cold day it was long walk for chilly stay in a dark place. In the summer the sun would shine through the cracks in the board walls and illuminate the spider webs that spanned the shadow dappled corners. I imagine even a truly inspired realtor would have a hard time coming up with a positive description of its dubious amenities.

Today our gleaming, tiled bathroom offers a

double occupancy whirlpool tub, glassed-in shower, his and hers sinks, gold fixtures, a large stained glass window, and a ten foot wide illuminated mirror that conceals three large "medicine" cabinets and twelve shelves loaded with personal miscellany. Oh, and a shut-the-door throne room for undisturbed reading—without spiders.

While we have two other bathrooms, the one I have just described is far more important, for this is where rituals take place that touch on our very souls. I think it has to do with the mirror and the secrets it holds.

They say that when a woman looks in a mirror she sees herself in infinitely fine detail. Hair by hair. Freckle by freckle, line by line, and pore by pore. Each of thousands of vital specifications are checked off against an internal scorecard that adds up to an impossibly high standard of female approval. (Including every other female in the hemisphere and also a few selected foreign cultures.)

On the other hand, a guy looks in the mirror and usually pronounces something to himself like, "Hey. Pretty damned good." If he happens to be standing next to the woman at that time, she will say, "You're not planning to wear that are you?"

This is not just theory. It was only a few years ago that I looked in the mirror and noticed that I had no eyebrows. No kidding. I'd gone my entire life not realizing that I had no real eyebrows. I've even gone back and looked old pictures. I can't say that I ever had any. Just a couple of kinky gray hairs above each eye that sprouted as, I think, the herald of old age.

What woman do you think would not notice it if her eyebrows went missing? What woman would not say to a friend in that condition, "Gwen, what did you do with your eyebrows?" Solely out of friendship and concern of course. No guy in my entire life ever mentioned that I'd come to work sans eyebrows.

A woman simply would not let this happen. They have a huge arsenal of resources at their disposal. Our little granddaughter, a toddler, has already investigated our bathroom drawers and attempted to put on lipstick.

Behind my side of the mirror my cabinet holds aspirin, super glue remover, eyeglass cleaner, six bottles of new and old prescriptions, vitamins, jock itch spray, Tums, shaving brush and soap, my razor, extra blades and the like.

The other side of our his and hers arrangement is twice the size of mine and holds, in addition to similar essentials, 48 bottles, tubes, flasks and jars of stuff whose purpose I can only guess at. Well, some are obvious, like hand lotions. But then there is Anti Gravity Mask, something that even NASA doesn't know about. I am not sure if she will be using this for a space walk she is planning or if she will soon be floating over the house like Mary Poppins, who had only an old fashioned umbrella.

Similarly there is also something in there called

Root Lifter Mousse." When my dad dynamited the huge stumps of giant trees left on our property, he still had to deal with the roots. He hired a guy with a bulldozer. Back then root lifter didn't come in a bottle. My gosh, it must be powerful stuff. Ditto the stuff called Skin Refinisher." When I bought Homer Formby's furniture refinisher at Ace Hardware it came with a warning to use it with rubber gloves. I hope she is careful with her version and doesn't get it on anything that is varnished.

My mom used to have a jar of cold cream, but I think that was about the extent of the magic potions. She didn't even have the one called Cucumber Heel Therapy, although I once did simulate the effect of it by stepping barefoot on dog poop on our lawn.

Stare deeply into the magic cabinet and fly away.

Lots of these things have French names. The French are famous for their cosmetics as well as not changing their underwear very often. So I hope they know what they're doing.

I've known Adriana since she was 13 years old. I thought she was beautiful then and she is still beautiful. I think most of that doesn't come from our bathroom shelves. She came home from the hairdresser's the other day and I complimented her on how her hair looked. She looked at me scornfully and told me that her hair guy had made a mistake in his schedule and couldn't do it. "Oh."

My father told me once, "Your mother is beautiful and it's on the inside." I've had the same kind of luck. Pretty good for a guy without eyebrows.

Dick

Seattle, Washington

> "I'm tired of all this nonsense about beauty being only skin-deep. That's deep enough. What do you want, an adorable pancreas?"
> —Jean Kerr

> **Adriana's KITCHEN**
> LA BUONA CUCINA
> di
> ADRIANA PAETZKE
>
> *Si mangia bene da noi*

You are where you eat

A fellow I know who'd lived in the Midwest told me about a sign he'd seen in a Michigan restaurant. "Restaurant" may be too fancy a word for the place he described. It sounded more like one of those highway-side diners with a flashing sign outside announcing "Eats." The sign inside, on the wall across from his stool at the counter, warned:

**IF YOU LOVE
HOME COOKING,
EAT AT HOME**

I've never been in Michigan, but somehow I am relatively certain that I've been in that restaurant—in fact, I think I've been there many times in many places. It's just one more of those places I have in that card catalog of dining experiences I carry around in the back of my mind.

I also have to confess that greasy spoons don't even rank near the bottom of my list—I've saved that for places of all kinds where you don't get treated well. There are days when one's body loudly cries out for a chili burger or a towering, jiggly hunk of lemon meringue pie and nothing else will do. I invariably feel remorse afterwards for eating that kind of stuff. It is a sort of self-flagellation that feels good when it stops, so places like that do have their role to play.

Back in the day when I was a young ad man ensconced in a downtown Seattle skyscraper, we had our choice of lunch venues that ranged from the Mirabeau, a ritzy French place up on our building's 50th floor, to bratwurst and booze at the old Rathskeller in the next block, to the Guadalajara's chalupas and beer in the heart of town, to Victor's 610 or the El Gaucho where ad agency and client people from all over gathered to drink too much and return late to work with their eyes unfocused. We tried them all. But I particularly remember one that was not on anybody's list.

No more than 50 yards from our building, kitty-corner across the street, was the unprepossessing entrance to the Hungerford Hotel and off in one corner its coffee shop. Built in 1928 the hotel hadn't kept pace with Seattle's burgeoning downtown core and looked shabby in comparison to its neighbors such as our glass-clad tower. Its coffee shop was just as worn, long, dim and narrow with a few tables and a row of booths down the side. The menu was simple, with predictable and more or less inexpensive dishes on the menu. The cook was hidden away somewhere in the back and the place was presided over at any given time by two or three waitresses who seemed to be interchangeable whether they were gaunt and gray haired old gals or plump, gray haired old gals. They somehow all wore the same look burnished by time and work and bore worthy, but no longer fashionable names like Mabel, Ethel, Ruby, Pearl or Louise.

 I recall sitting in a booth with a young art director named Jerry who worked for me and another fellow out of the creative department whose name or face I can no longer summon up. We'd ordered and were eating and talking. Across from me Jerry sat turned sideways in the booth with one foot on the worn and cracked red vinyl bench. Suddenly one of the Mabels appeared and slapped his knee off the bench. "Get your foot off that seat young man," she demanded. "Your mother wouldn't let you sit like that home!"

 We all looked at one another and hung our heads in shame. I guess we weren't as grown up and sophisticated in that environment as we thought we were in other places. We didn't get home cooking in that coffee shop, but we sure got a taste of home. Maybe that's somehow why it seemed so comfortable. If any of those Mabels still lived today, and I knew where to find them, I think I would send them a Mother's Day card.

Other restaurants, waiters and waitresses have stood out, too—mostly for the wrong reasons. On a recent cruise through the Hawaiian Islands we paid extra not to eat in the main dining salon, but to dine instead in one of the upper scale specialty restaurants on board. We had to make reservations for it almost a week in advance on the ten day trip. The place was dripping with ambience and had a lovely menu listing much trendy chow and expensive wines. Our waiter introduced himself. "Hi, I'm Troy; I'll be your server." In one minute he was intimate with us. We'd just started chewing when he was there with, "How is everything?"

"Mmm. Mmmf," we answered. More chatter came with the main course and the wine. What had started out as *our* special evening added a third and uninvited party. I can't remember what the food was, but I still remember the waiter. I should have taken his picture for our memory book. As we were still eating the parts of our dinner that we'd both saved for the last and best savory bites, and drinking from still half filled glasses, he arrived to hover over us while he tentatively reached for our plates and asked, "Are you guys still workin' on that?"

We snatched our plates and glasses out of his grasp. I can still hear that "Are you guys still workin' on that?" As I write this, I am struggling not to grind my teeth and clench my fists. In our favorite places, dinner is to linger over and good tastes are to be drawn and relished. Wine and conversation and the joy of dining aren't a "job" that must be completed. It isn't that way everywhere. Italian waiters are born understanding that and watch from a distance until a gesture or a nod tells them you need something or are ready for your check. They learn from their fathers and their pride comes from your joy in your dining experience. That's true in Europe and much of the rest of the world.

Ruggero Taradel, a historian and author raised in Rome, told me he was astounded after coming to America to discover that waiters here will frequently kneel alongside guests at the table as though they expect to be petted on their heads. Adriana told me they do it to get down even with you at eye level. This is apparently a form of egalitarian democracy they impose on you, so they can be your best friend instead of your waiter. "In Italy," Ruggero said, "it would simply get them immediately fired and you'd get an apology from the manager." What a wonderful idea.

That's not to say there are not wonderful restaurants, fine waiters and superb dining here at home. However, even though I haven't been all over the world, I think some things here are slipping because of our "everything goes" culture. My hearing isn't so hot, but it is clear to me that more American women than ever are screaming in restaurants and shrieking with laughter like drunken fraternity boys. More men are wearing baseball caps while they eat.

(They need more Mabels to slap them off their heads and remind them of what their mothers taught them.) More people are sharing loudmouth cell phone conversations with the entire room. More parents are letting themselves and people at nearby tables be dominated by the rude behavior of children who don't know better. And far too many waiters and waitresses still seem compelled to ask, "Are you still workin' on that?" Is there a waiter school somewhere that teaches them that?

There is a place near us called the Wedgwood Broiler. It's been around as long as I can remember and recently earned a special honor in a handsome, yuppified magazine called Seattle Metropolitan as a "Classic Restaurant." Its customers all used to have a lot of gray hair. Now more and more young families and younger people are going there, perhaps because it is a good value and stands in stark contrast to places that serve nouvelle cuisine, "small plates" and tapas—all miniscule servings of designer food at huge prices that leave you both hungry and broke. (What a reward for handing somebody your money.)

At the Wedgwood Broiler, many of the waitresses have no longer fashionable names like Mabel, Ethel, Ruby, Pearl or Louise. Some have been there for 20 years. The food is honest, straightforward and good and we enjoy it. But it's not home cooking.

For that you can't beat Adriana's Kitchen: Scrumptious Italian *sartú di riso*, fork-tender pot roast, Chicken Divan, and lifesaving *pasta in brodo* like her grandmother used to make when people didn't feel so hot. If you love home cooking, eat at home. It's best when you and the cook are in love. And you don't put your feet on the furniture.

Dick

Seattle, Washington

"Mable, Mable, sweet and able,
Get your elbows off the table..."
—A song fragment hanging around from times gone by.

The Trojan horse

Here in Troy we weren't really prepared for the invasion. We were living in a kind of dream state, I guess.

Well before Saturday, Adriana had brought the horse into our family room. It had been stashed away in a part of our attic only accessible through a cabinet door in our bedroom wall. That door opens into a storage area crammed with blankets and pillows and things we rarely use.

In the back of that, behind all that never-thought-about stuff, is another door leading into the attic itself, a hotly stuffy, barren space where the joists of the ceiling below are battened with itchy fiberglass insulation and where you have to inch along on your hands and knees so you don't bang your head on the roof rafters. It was a perfect spot to tuck away Childhood Things That Must Be Kept. The horse had been in that category for the last 28 years. (My wife will throw away my favorite shirts just when they've gotten nicely broken in, but some things are immune to her zeal.)

It was worth all the taking out and putting back. Giordana was coming. For some reason, her selfish parents want to keep their child to themselves for most days, but we can occasionally pry her free from their greedy clutches.

We'd been waiting for Saturday to have her overnight. It was like a gift. Of course the Trojans thought that the horse Odysseus had left at their city's gates was a gift too. Up to that point they had never heard the expression, "beware of Greeks bearing gifts." When they opened the gates, the sky fell in on them.

Giordana isn't yet three feet tall. But she makes a tornado look like a mild summer zephyr. It's not her fault, it's ours. Or maybe mine because I cannot resist her. The rocking horse was obviously hers from the minute she saw it and she was determined ride it like Ghengis Khan in wild conquest of her territory. But before she had even climbed on its back, she had to round up her allies. She rushed up the stairs to the bedroom where her crib and other essentials waited. (Rushing upstairs is, in itself, no mean task when the stair treads come halfway to your waist.) She gathered everything she needed for personal

happiness and brought it downstairs in a half dozen trips—a remarkable feat that reminded me of Egyptians moving giant rocks to build the pyramids:
1. A teddy bear that talks, sings, and recites.
2. A teddy bear holding an I Love You heart.
3. A teddy bear that does nothing .
4. A soft gadget hung above her crib that plays music as it revolves.
5. A fuzzy pink pig that oinks and wrinkles its snout as it walks across the floor.
6. A rubber ball in the shape of a world globe.
7. A child-sized baseball bat.
8. Five soft cubes with little stuffed figures inside.
9. A toy cell phone that rings and lights up.
10. Eleven story books in English and Italian.
11. A kid-sized roll-aboard suitcase.
12. A tiny child's purse with a compact, coin purse and another cell phone.
13. Assorted Lego® pieces.
14. A gigantic plastic push-around thing that makes bizarre sound effects and music as you push it.
15. A tin tea set with cups, saucers, plates, teapot and tray in a suitcase-style case.
16. A heavy wooden puzzle with farm animals that fit into farm-animal-shaped holes.
17. An Italian book with buttons to push that make animal sounds.
18. A wooden dog pull toy.

19. Five plastic rings of different sizes stacked on a post.
20. *Plus* two grungy and well-used duck decoys from the garage.

All this was piled onto the family room sofa, chairs, and coffee table and overflowed onto the floor. It was immediately disregarded as her next strategic move was to the cabinet with the TV, DVD and CD systems. There she began pushing buttons while pantomiming dancing and loudly demanding her favorite music (which we wisely keep pre-loaded in the changer.) Twirling round and round until she got dizzy, she then staggered into the kitchen and invaded her favorite drawer, the one with all the plastic containers. Withdrawing a baby bottle, she filled it from the dog's water dish and began to drink until Adriana's horrified screaming temporarily diverted her from her mini-mission of chaos.

Abandoning her dog water refreshment center, she waddled happily back to the family room throwing four plastic balls in all directions. Soon there was only one, the other three being under the armoire, the sofa, and missing without a trace, respectively. When I went into the garage to bend a coat hanger into a hook to retrieve two of the balls, I turned to find her right behind me trying to attach a 1/2" socket to a greasy ratchet wrench, apparently for a future project she had in mind.

She then spotted a heavy mechanic's stool with wheels and a swiveling seat that she dragged into the family room to play merry-go-round on and push wildly around the room squealing with the unrestrained joy of a baby barbarian sacking a fallen and helpless city.

Her conquest of our formerly quiet space was interrupted by a trip to the grocery store to reload with bananas after she had eaten the three we had at home. That may sound gluttonous, but even conquerors have their soft spots and she had generously shared her snack with the dog, tossing chunks of banana down from the heights of her high chair with one hand while she was busily spooning lunch in the general direction of her face with the other. Those bibs with a pocket at the bottom are marvelous inventions!

After that it was time for her to address her minions. She commandeered my lap and tried to reach her cohorts by telephone in my office, a handset in each hand as she blabbered into their mouthpieces. Failing a response she tried the handset on my fax machine. An hour later we found our home phone line out of order, dead with no dial tone. I called the phone company for a service call, only to discover the fax phone off the hook and the fax basket filled with story books. I canceled the service call. Clever sabotage.

Speech making came next as she streaked around the family room pursued by a wildly barking dog, perhaps one of her personal advisers. We thought maybe she would be addressing her submissive subjects in Italian since Adriana has assiduously worked at teaching her that lovely language. But no, she was shouting, "Quack, quack," as she carried around a solid wood antique duck decoy she had liberated from an end table. It has taken weeks for her grandmother to teach her *mangia, aqua, nonno, grazie* and *cane*. It took only one trip to the zoo to teach her "Quack, Quack," a terrifying war cry.

Frankly, we gave up without much of a fight. The mighty midget is a powerful individual. I heard her screaming upstairs, "Nonno, Nonno" or something close to that. I rushed to the staircase to find her teetering at the top step clutching Vearl Ferguson, a large pig carved of solid Philipine mahogany, two-thirds her size and weighing one-third of what she does. I fielded the two of them as they were about to plunge down the stairs.

The siege lasted only a few hours. It ended when the mini-conqueror pooped her diaper and then blissfully went to sleep before her parents came.

Adriana, the Helen of our Troy, sighed. I stared numbly after the departing car. We both realized we were victims of the Stockholm Syndrome, so-called after an incident where hostages displayed misplaced loyalty and emotional attachment to the fellow holding them at gunpoint in a Swedish bank.

We held hands as we turned to one another sadly admitting the uncomfortable truth to ourselves—we'd fallen in love with our captor.

Even the spectacularly incautious Trojans weren't that sappy.

Dick
Seattle, Washington

Historical Note: The original invaders of Troy did not come equipped with nearly as much stuff.

Acknowledgements

Many thanks to Steven McMacken, master graphic designer and painter of things Hawaiian for his handsome cover design, painstaking proofreading and effort to visually showcase my words. I'm grateful to Juliet Shen as well for her professional guidance on typography in the interior text. I equally appreciate all those friends who pored over my original manuscripts and tested my thoughts and words against their own tastes and expertise to help me make this little book better. I'm also indebted to the editors of the Washington Athletic Club Magazine for their kind permission to re-publish two stories, *The Advent* and *Whatever Happened to the Holidays?* that previously appeared in their pages and are now Postcards. Most importantly of all, thank you, my beloved Adriana, for your loving and insightful suggestions and endless encouragement that made this book possible.

Finally, errors of fact and intolerable exaggerations should be laid at nobody's doorstep other than my own, although I claim some small measure of artistic license and I hope therefore immunity.

About the author

Dick Paetzke is a longtime advertising agency creative director and writer as well as head of his own creative services business A native of Seattle, Washington, he has been an infantry soldier, hobby dog trainer, cold and shivering duck hunter, student of languages, amateur photographer, songwriter, stepfather, ardent reader, motor scooter rider, novice grandfather, author, and fancier of well-cooked pot roast. He makes his home in Seattle and Lecce, Italy with his wife, Adriana.

Please feel free to contact me at postcardsbook@comcast.net. I welcome your questions, thoughts, ideas and opinions.
—*Dick Paetzke*

GLOW WORM
Written by Paul Lincke, Johnny Mercer and Lilla Robinson. Used by permission of Edward B. Marks Music Company.